■ Advance Praise for ■
Ministry with Prisoners & Families: The Way Forward

"This book puts communities of faith on the front lines of a battle for the dawn of a new day. If you choose to read one book on the wretched state of the criminal justice system today and its devastating effects on the family and on our communities, especially among the poor, this book is a must have. The writers provide the church with unprecedented opportunities to rise up and offer the world the answers we have had along—the truth of God's Word and the love of God's people."

—Dr. H. David Schuringa, President,
Crossroad Bible Institute, Grand Rapids, Michigan

"Finally, a book that equips churches to minister more effectively to those affected by incarceration! These authors give us the benefit of their many decades of experience and study. Learn from them before you begin your prison-related ministry. If you are already engaged in this kind of ministry, stop what you are doing and read this book."

—Joseph Williams, President,
Christian Association for Prison Aftercare

"*Ministry with Prisoners & Families* will be important in helping to break the cycle of incarceration and recidivism, especially with the authors' focus on the family as a critical element. The book provides a realistic, practical approach to addressing the problem of incarceration that will restore lives, reunite families, and rebuild communities. It is a must-read for churches, reentry programs, and the corrections community."

—Rev. Carmen Warner-Robbins, MSN, RN, MDiv,
FAAN, CEO and Founder, Welcome Home Ministries

"Nearly every criminal justice expert acknowledges the disproportionate number of minorities that populate our nation's prisons and jails. This book doesn't merely lament that fact; it offers sound direction and biblically grounded ministry practices that can alter the future of those men and women caught in the web of incarceration. Written primarily to challenge African American churches to form healing communities of support for offenders and their families, it in fact sounds a call for all congregations that take seriously their mandate to 'remember those in prison.' Every pastor, along with anyone engaged in prison or jail ministry, should carefully read and prayerfully consider the principles presented in this book."

—W. Thomas Beckner, PhD, Associate Professor of Criminal Justice, Department of Criminal Justice, Psychology and Social Science, Trine University

Ministry with Prisoners & Families
THE WAY FORWARD

W. Wilson Goode Sr. ■ Charles E. Lewis Jr. ■ Harold Dean Trulear

FOREWORD BY ADDIE RICHBURG

AFTERWORD BY DEEDEE M. COLEMAN

JUDSON PRESS
PUBLISHERS SINCE 1824
VALLEY FORGE, PA

Ministry with Prisoners & Families: The Way Forward

Judson Press has made every effort to trace the ownership of all quotes. In the event of a question arising from the use of a quote, we regret any error made and will be pleased to make the necessary correction in future printings and editions of this book.

Unless otherwise indicated, Scripture quotations are from the *New Revised Standard Version of the Bible*, copyrighted 1989 by the Division of Christian Education of the National Council of Christ in the United States of America, and are used by permission. All rights reserved.

Scripture quotations marked NIV are taken from the Holy Bible, New International Version®, NIV®. Copyright © 1973, 1978, 1984, 2010 by Biblica, Inc.TM Used by permission of Zondervan. All rights reserved worldwide.

Scripture quotations marked KJV are from *The Holy Bible*, King James Version.

Scripture quotations marked NLT are from the *Holy Bible*, New Living Translation, copyright © 1996, 2004. Used by permission of Tyndale House Publishers, Inc., Wheaton, IL 60189. All rights reserved.

Interior design by Crystal Devine. Cover art by Dane Tilghman.

Library of Congress Cataloging-in-Publication data

Ministry with prisoners & families : the way forward / [edited by] W. Wilson Goode, Sr., Charles E. Lewis, Jr., Harold Dean Trulear. -- 1st ed.
    p. cm.
  ISBN 978-0-8170-1664-7 (pbk. : alk. paper) 1. Church work with African American families. 2. Church work with prisoners. 3. Church work with criminals. 4. African Americans--Religion. I. Goode, W. Wilson. II. Lewis, Charles E. III. Trulear, Harold Dean.
  BV4468.2.A34M56 2011
  259'.508996073--dc22
                        2010051786

Printed in the U.S.A.
First Edition, 2011.

Contents

Foreword

David Lowes Watson, a contemporary Wesleyan scholar and professor at Wesley Theological Seminary in Washington, DC, suggests that "acts of compassion" and "acts of justice" may be a more contemporary translation of the "works of mercy" in their personal and social forms. This comes together in *Ministry with Prisoners & Families: The Way Forward.*

As President of the National Alliance of Faith and Justice, I found that each author in this volume captured the concerns of the past decade with vivid accuracy. Like the individual verses of a beloved hymn or favorite song, the message of each contributor speaks differently to each reader, but all work in harmony and repeats around a central refrain. The book creates a call and response of voices, and each contributor speaks from the passion of authority rooted in personal and credentialed experience, and many connect that authority with a theological appeal.

I was moved by the writing of Ms. Alfreda Robinson-Dawkins, who welcomed readers into the sanctity of her valley experience and of her struggles and victories post-release. Her story is a truthful reminder that our own human failings should transform judgmental attitudes into compassion toward those who are convicted of an offense.

Dr. Wilson Goode's valuable chapter outlines the progression of federal support for mentoring children of prisoners—an issue developed further elsewhere in the book, calling for engagement of the black church in legislative development. Church involvement is needed, not solely in responding to legislation after it is made law, but more critically in recommending new policies that favor restoration for returning citizens.

Dr. Keith Reeves skillfully navigates post–civil rights inequities in his chapter's remarkable analysis of youthful black males. He offers a direct challenge to the black church to become the epicenter for multisystem partnership in the midst of this crisis. Such partnerships are complex, and Dr. Reeves outlines many points on which to base this discussion.

I particularly noted Chaplain Michael Smith's contribution about prison chaplains, a role held dear by Rev. Warren Dolphus, my late husband and retired chaplain with the Bureau of Prisons. Chaplain Smith captures the relationship between the church, those imprisoned, and their families, and the possibilities in that relationship, possibilities which led Chaplain Dolphus and I to cofound the National Alliance of Faith and Justice more than ten years ago.

Dr. Harold Dean Trulear raises one of the most important questions in the book by asking, *"How can we take what we already have and do, and mobilize it to better serve this population?"* The compartmentalization of prison ministry to a category reserved for "the faithful few" rather than the priority of the entire church is in fact a question of our *FAITH*—facilitating assistance in transition and healing.

All in all, contributions to this book underscore lyrics in Charles Wesley's timeless hymn, "A Charge To Keep I Have," lyrics based on this passage from Matthew Henry's classic commentary on Leviticus: "We have every one of us a charge to keep, an eternal God to glorify, an immortal soul to provide for, needful duty to be done, our generation to serve; and it must be our daily care to keep this charge...."

In these words, we find a foundation for this rich resource and the challenge of each author's appeal: We have a charge to keep and immortal souls for whom to provide—the souls of prisoners, returning citizens, and their families. This ministry is the duty of every person who recognizes Christ as Lord, and in this book, disciples of Jesus will find a way forward.

Addie L. Richburg
President and CEO

Acknowledgments

The editors and contributors wish to acknowledge the support of the Annie E. Casey Foundation and of program officer Carole Thompson, whose support of the Howard University School of Divinity lecture series and workshops on ministry with families of the incarcerated provided much of the material for this book.

Introduction

W. WILSON GOODE SR., CHARLES E. LEWIS JR.,
AND HAROLD DEAN TRULEAR

There is a crisis in our criminal justice system today, a crisis African American churches must not ignore. We see the crisis in millions of lives in our communities that are affected by crime and the justice system. We experience it in the disproportionate number of African Americans currently incarcerated in our nation's jails and prisons. The crisis swells as we consider the numbers of children, spouses, mothers, fathers, sisters, brothers, and significant others left behind to deal with grief, anger, separation, and shame. The crisis becomes a tidal wave as we consider projections pointing toward an ever-increasing number of prisons under construction due to underachievement of inner-city and poor children in today's elementary schools.

God and God's church should have a word for those affected by tidal waves. This book addresses the critical need for African American churches to respond to this crisis by ministering to the needs of incarcerated persons and their families. In this critical moment, God has placed an opportunity before congregations serving the African American community. Our congregations have been given a chance—perhaps a "second chance"—to become involved in the forefront of building the commonwealth of God.

The problems of crime and incarceration loom large in America. However, our nation's record incarceration rates do not impact all neighborhoods equally. A disproportionate number of African Americans and other people of color are being sent to our nation's jails and prisons. Similarly, the challenges of reentry for those returning from incarceration impact neighborhoods differently as well. Disproportionately, it is African Americans released from incarceration and returning to low-income neighborhoods with limited resources to support their reintegration that pose the greatest challenge.

This text argues that congregations can help break the cycle of crime, recidivism, and intergenerational incarceration. Shalom, true peace, requires more than what the legal system's institutional responses of incarceration, rehabilitation, and reentry services can provide. Through prison ministries that build relationships, ministries to families of the incarcerated, reentry ministries that lead to reintegration, and informed and prayerful policy advocacy, African American churches can and do play significant roles in bringing about shalom for communities affected by crime and incarceration.

The prison system extracts valuable resources from neighborhoods, families, and victims, weakening the community infrastructure. In order to reverse the tide of mass incarceration, people of faith must surround those affected by incarceration with what the Annie E. Casey Foundation calls a "healing community."[1] African American churches possess the values and commitment to redemption and healing that position them to be catalysts for such a transformation. They also specialize in building relationships of forgiveness and restoration that enable individuals to satisfy their God-created destiny to belong to something and someone significant.

Sobering Statistics

The most recent numbers on incarceration and prisoner reentry speak to the urgent need. The United States incarcerates its citizens at the highest rate of any nation. The U.S. Bureau of Justice Statistics reports that at midyear 2008 more than 2.3 million people were being held in federal or state prisons or in local jails. From 2000 to 2007, the overall prison population grew annually by an average of 2.4 percent. An additional 7 million persons are under the supervision of probation or parole.[2]

Data from the Pew Center confirm that the situation is especially daunting among African Americans. Currently, 1 in 15 African American males over age eighteen is behind bars, as opposed to 1 of every 36 Latinos and 1 of 106 white males. In addition, the Center reports that one of every nine African American males between the ages of 25 and 34 is behind bars.[3]

The U.S. Department of Justice states that approximately 650,000 men and women are released from state and federal prisons annually—and this number does not include the many others who come home after release from city and county jails. Each year our communities are flooded with people returning from incarceration, having been worn down by isolation, degradation, and warehousing. The vast majority of these individuals return to communities already in distress due to poverty, weak infrastructure, and limited institutional development. Yet these same communities are home to a variety of houses of worship that can and do provide social and religious resources to support people in the reentry process. And in this fact, there is hope.

Finding Hope in the Scriptures

The Scriptures remind us there is hope. When the prophet Isaiah saw a flood, he saw the presence of God. Through Isaiah, the Lord reminded his people: "When you pass through the waters, I will be with you; and through the rivers, they shall not overwhelm you" (Isaiah 43:2). In the same way, God is present, by his Spirit and in the church, for those affected by incarceration. This collection of essays and articles speaks about the ways in which God's presence is being made manifest through the church in its ministries to and among those most affected by crime and incarceration. We are making the case for how congregations, specifically those serving the African American community, can develop a vision for prison ministry that moves beyond a few church members stopping by a correctional facility to lead an occasional Bible study or worship service. We're encouraging churches to have a significant presence in the lives of men, women, and youth who are (1) incarcerated, (2) returning from incarceration, (3) at risk of incarceration, or (4) dealing with a family member's incarceration. We consistently address the key theme of relationship building as the core of working with this population. In the words of Rev. Michael Smith, a contributor to this text who serves as a chaplain in the Federal Bureau of Prisons, "Prison ministry is more than a worship service. It is more than a Bible and a tambourine." Rather, it is the essence of church itself.

We contend that congregations should treat prison ministry and incarceration the same way they do ministry to the sick and hospitalization. When a church member is ill, certain members of the congregation, such as deacons and the like, may be assigned to visit—but the caregiving function does not rest solely with "specialized ministries." Rather, the whole church springs to action—visiting the sick, looking after the family, providing rides to the hospital, preparing meals— offering whatever the individual and family needs in its season of distress. Why shouldn't the church respond similarly when a person is arrested or incarcerated? Why should ministry to these individuals and their families (if it occurs at all) be confined to a small group of "prison ministry" people in a congregation? What if the whole congregation saw its role as providing ministry and support for the incarcerated and their families as they do the sick and their kin? After all, Jesus included the sick and imprisoned in the same list in Matthew 25.

As we will see in the pages that follow, a fully orbed prison ministry approaches the reality of incarceration just as it does the ordeal of illness. Not only does it involve the mobilization of congregational resources in such areas as visitation, consolation, and support, but it also requires better understanding of the culture of the institutions housing the persons to whom we minister. Church members know how to interact with someone in a hospital room. We can learn how to interact with someone behind bars. We know how to comfort a family during a terminal illness. We should know how to provide support to a mother grieving the incarceration of her son and struggling with the stigma and shame associated with his incarceration. We've learned to interact with medical professionals when a church member is hospitalized. We must learn to interact with correctional, probation, and parole officials as we seek to stake out the presence of God amid the criminal justice flood.

In that same vein, we need to learn to access support for needs we cannot meet ourselves. When a person returns from incarceration, he or she may have needs we cannot meet—finding a job or housing, for example. But we can build networks with those who can help meet these needs, and accompany our friends on their trips to those agencies that can provide assistance. And we can be a supportive presence when the needed services are delayed or do not materialize—when finding the job seems impossible, housing is nonexistent, and the enormity of the adjustment feels unbearable. In these times, the church can and should be present as a primary means of support for individuals and families.

We base this support-building process in the concrete realities of family and community relationships. Some experts estimate that each inmate connects directly with fourteen individuals—family members, friends, employers, even victims. A holistic ministry to those returning from incarceration cannot ignore those connections. These individuals are in need of the restoration of relationships; some are virtually beginning anew in their attempts to really connect with others.

Finding Hope in History

The history of incarceration in the United States cannot be written apart from the hope the church provided amid the reality of prison and jail from the early days of the republic. In the 1800s, the prison chaplain played a primary role in efforts at the rehabilitation of prisoners. Chaplains visited inmates, offered counsel and sermons, and even served as librarians and teachers—all in hopes that change would come about.[4] Indeed, the hope for change in incarceration—real spiritual change—gave rise to the creation of a new type of prison known as a "penitentiary," in which inmates were sentenced ostensibly to have time in solitude to contemplate the error of their ways and "repent."[5] Many Christians loaned their support to such a philosophy of incarceration. It is no coincidence that the focus on solitude and repentance became staples at the first major U.S. penitentiary, built in Quaker-influenced Philadelphia in 1829.

As the 1800s drew to a close, the relative ineffectiveness of the penitentiary system and the growing secularity of the nation led to a shift in the American philosophy of incarceration. Growing secularism saw repentance give way to rehabilitation, and the "penitentiary" became a "house of corrections." Change was still the goal, but the change was no longer clearly related to religious or spiritual matters. The role of chaplains similarly shifted: "With the rise of rationalism and scientific positivism, the chaplain became a religious representative in a secularized institution of professionals. As a consequence, the chaplaincy was marginalized as religion moved from the center of penology to its periphery."[6] Chaplains' duties in education and other fields were taken over by secular professionals, and their ministry goals were shifted to fit the new standards of rehabilitation developed in a secular context. Yet chaplains persist through to this day, providing religious services in this more marginalized role. The wonder may be that with the trivialization of religion in the postmodern world, chaplains have as much influence as they do.

So history teaches us that (1) religious faith contributed mightily to the genesis of the American penal system and its philosophy, and (2) even when society marginalizes religious faith, faith persists as a force within the prison walls. This book is a call to join and expand that history with renewed vision and commitment.

Prison Ministry Today

Moving forward, we offer several key concepts that require the churches' understanding in developing an engagement strategy for prison ministry in order to serve this present age:

1. *We affirm a continuum between prison ministry and ministry to those reentering society from incarceration.* Whether working in a long-term prison facility or a short-term jail, we must be mindful that most inmates will return to society. Between America's prisons and jails, we can expect approximately 95 percent of incarcerated individuals to return home at some point.[7] The question for congregations in prison ministry becomes, "Does our ministry to incarcerated individuals end with their release?" Obviously, it does not—just as our care for the sick doesn't end the moment they are released from the hospital. Yet many congregations that minister in prisons and jails give little attention to ministry among the same individuals after their release. The inconsistency of such a truncated approach presses us to call for prison ministries to follow through with their charges subsequent to release. Ideally, the focus on reentry begins the moment a person is sentenced—thinking through a plan that will keep inmates in contact with their families over the course of

the incarceration. Plans should be made for activities behind bars that will better prepare them for their return to society. This is as much a matter of the heart (contrition and repentance) as it is of the head (developing useful skills). Similarly, those who would minister successfully to those returning from incarceration must, by definition, also be involved in prison ministry, since the process of reentry and reengagement begins during incarceration. The logic is inescapable: Good prison ministry gives attention to reentry, and good reentry ministry requires prison ministry.

2. *We offer a new, theologically informed definition of the person returning from incarceration: the "returning citizen."* This term arose from the dissatisfaction of religious and civic leaders in Detroit with the term "ex-offender." They sought new language that would better reflect the hope of reintegrating people into the community rather than underlining the stigma that surrounds incarceration. Such renaming of persons formerly incarcerated resists the tendencies in popular culture and civic discourse to objectify, marginalize, and dehumanize such persons. Rev. Lonnie McLeod, a Harlem pastor and contributor to this text who began his theological education in the famed Sing Sing program of New York Theological Seminary,[8] reflects a similar philosophy when he urges: "Don't define me by what I was—define me as who I am. How would you like it if you were introduced publicly in terms of the worst period of your life?"[9] Additionally, this new terminology challenges the validity of "collateral sanctions"—laws and policies that limit opportunities for returning citizens subsequent to their release, such as restrictions on housing, voting, education, and employment. (We will cover these in more detail in this book's chapter on policy and barriers to reentry.) Suffice it to say that the church must challenge such policies when they appear unjust and avoid cooperating with stigmatization in our own reference to the population we serve in Christ's name.

3. *We believe ministry to those affected by crime and criminal justice must move beyond simply addressing the plight of the incarcerated. Other key stakeholders in the mix include family members, friends, the communities to which they return, and those victimized by their behavior.* We are just beginning to recognize fully the impact of incarceration on the families of individuals in jails and prisons.[10] When a family member is incarcerated, the family faces economic issues, changes to parenting structures, the trauma of separation, and the stigma and shame surrounding incarceration itself.

Children are particularly vulnerable when a parent is incarcerated, as they often experience not only separation from the parent, but also severance from siblings and displacement to different caregivers. Children with parents behind bars are more likely to experience poverty, parental substance abuse and mental illness, and other associated risk factors. They are also at greater risk for alcohol and drug abuse, poor academic performance, and juvenile delinquency and other factors that increase their probability of being incarcerated at some point in time.

The stigma and shame of incarceration looms large in congregations where many members have family who are incarcerated, be they spouses, children, parents, or others. Many in the church feel ashamed or ostracized when they disclose the incarceration of an immediate family member, and instead employ euphemisms not unlike those once used for out-of-wedlock pregnancies in the black community, saying the family member is "away with relatives" or "down South." Family members may even say a relative is "at school" or "in the service" as a way of offering a quick explanation to inquiring minds while avoiding the isolation and shame that accompany incarceration.

We believe that congregations can begin to reduce the shame and stigma of incarceration by naming the reality. Incarceration affects all of our communities. There are very few congregations in the African American community (or for that matter, in America in general) that do not contain at least one household dealing with the reality of incarceration in their family, irrespective of class or location. For congregations to become mobilized around prison ministry and reentry, they must create safe space for families to speak about the ways the issue affects them, from the pulpit to the door.[11] Breaking the silence on incarceration means moving beyond talking about it as a "black issue" to embracing it as a personal and communal issue. Incarceration moves from the third person to the first person, and we must own it as a reality that affects the lives of our church members—and even our church leaders.

By naming incarceration as a family issue, we can walk with family members during the time of separation from their loved one(s). We support caregivers left behind to raise children and grandchildren; we provide listening ears as they rehearse their struggles; and we make sure they hear their story in the gospel story—the story of a man who gave his life for them while in custody! Throughout this book we treat prison ministry and prisoner reentry as family and relational issues. We affirm the need for one-on-one mentoring and discipleship of those who are incarcerated. But we recognize that their lives are inextricably tied to others who deserve our attention as well.

4. *We believe congregations must understand the differences between prisons and jails, and recognize the different ministry needs in each.* Prisons are part of either the state or federal system and generally house inmates serving terms of a year or more. Jails are normally operated by cities or counties and house inmates who are serving short-term sentences or awaiting trial or sentencing. The distinction is critical. While congregations working in prisons can seek to build long-term relationships with inmates, the populations at jails are, by definition, far more transient and require a ministry approach

that recognizes "they ain't got long to stay here." Congregations working in jails should be aware that many of the men, women, and juveniles with whom they are ministering will be returning home soon—often to the communities where the congregations themselves serve. This means that congregations that are working with short-term facilities must be even more attentive to reentry ministries.

5. *Finally, we affirm that prison ministry requires both service and advocacy.* The prisoner needs not only ministries of care and support, but also the prophetic voice of the church that speaks truth to power regarding the difficulties of rehabilitation, transformation, and reintegration. With radical cutbacks in funding for the provision of social services, even the noble goals of the secular rehabilitation agenda lay beyond the reach of many inmates. The challenges of prison overcrowding, sentencing disparity, economic hardship, and limited resources for education, substance abuse treatment, and vocational training all directly affect the quality of life for inmates and their families. Collateral sanctions can overwhelm individuals and families during the reentry period. Congregations must develop advocacy ministries that speak to the systemic realities that make successful rehabilitation, transformation, and reintegration possible. One reason the transitions involved in reentry overwhelm individuals and families is because much of our ministry to this population is service-based with little advocacy. We need to be better informed of the policies, laws, and regulations that govern the lives of the incarcerated, and support those that fit the demands of justice, but also temper justice with mercy to bring about conditions that lead to transformation and reintegration. We spend time in this text pointing toward some of the policy issues that require our attention in this age. We also offer suggestions with regard to how congregations can be more effective voices for those affected by incarceration and their families.

About This Book

The book begins with several chapters that provide introductory material on the subject of prison ministry. Chapter 1 is an overview of African Americans and the criminal justice system by Charles E. Lewis Jr., former professor at Howard University School of Social Work. Lewis lays out the challenges presented by the disproportionate numbers of African Americans incarcerated in our country, considers questions of access to justice, education, and human services for high risk populations, and gives attention to concerns regarding juvenile justice in the black community. The second chapter, authored by Karen Swanson, director of the Institute for Prison Ministry at the Billy Graham Center–Wheaton College, focuses on the training and educational needs of both professionals and volunteers involved in what she calls "Christian Correctional Ministry." Dr. Swanson argues for a new level of excellence in ministry in both prisons and jails, formation for the specific roles of professionals and volunteers in correctional ministry, and the need for a holistic approach that considers all persons affected by crime and incarceration. In chapter 3, Swarthmore College political scientist Keith Reeves reports on the culture and decision-making processes of African American males who are incarcerated in several state correctional facilities. Using data from his research and that of the *Washington Post*, Reeves considers the thought processes, means of coping, and relational skills of young African American males in prison. He specifically focuses on the decision-making processes that led to their incarceration and ways in which the resources of congregations (both relational and ideational) can be directed toward transformation.

The second section of the book covers a wide variety of specific issues within the general framework of ministry to persons affected by incarceration. In chapter 4, Pastor Owen Cardwell focuses on how churches can support "family

connectivity"—helping families stay connected through written and verbal communication and visitation while a family member is incarcerated and then supporting both returning citizens and their families during the reentry transition.
Cardwell also lays forth the biblical basis for family connectivity and prison ministry and offers suggestions for congregational response. In chapter 5, we move from keeping
families together to supporting children, as Wilson Goode
introduces the Amachi Mentoring Model, a nationally recognized ministry that works directly with children of the incarcerated. This chapter focuses on how congregations, through
mentoring, provide a support system for children separated
from their incarcerated parents. In chapter 6, Dr. Deborah
Jackson Meyers profiles another family-oriented model that
seeks to break the chain of incarceration across the generations by offering a variety of supplementary services to children of the incarcerated, including mentoring, tutoring, and
sponsorship. She also identifies ways churches can partner
with other community and educational agencies that support
children of the incarcerated and their families.

Black women constitute the fastest-growing population
in U.S. prisons today. In chapter 7, the African American
church's ministry to these women receives specific attention
from Alfreda Robinson, executive director of the National
Women's Prison Project. She presses the church to look at the
distinct situations and risk factors that contribute to female
involvement in the criminal justice system, the impact on the
lives of families and children, and the role congregations can
play in being communities of support. Robinson draws on
her experience, giving special attention to the way relational
issues often shape the decision-making processes of women
who become incarcerated and the way healthy relationships
can lead them down the road of successful reintegration.

The next three chapters consider the role of social and
mental health services in ministry with those affected by crime
and criminal justice. In chapter 8, Charles E. Lewis Jr. speaks

to the psychological, emotional, and behavioral health needs of African American youth, exploring preventative, alternative, and supplemental measures to minister to at-risk youth. Because congregations are often the first line of defense in addressing mental health issues in the black community (as opposed to secular mental health service providers), it is important that congregational leadership understand both the critical role they play as providers and the need for networking to access professional services in mental health. In chapter 9, Rev. Sylvia Moseley Robinson addresses the relationship between substance abuse and incarceration. Research indicates that more than two-thirds of America's prison and jail population had some type of drug or alcohol problem at the time they were incarcerated. Moseley Robinson explores ways congregations can incorporate evidence-based intervention and treatment strategies both within the local church and in partnership with treatment professionals, and also offers a biblical model for ministering to those struggling with addictions. Meanwhile, in chapter 10, Dr. Veronica Lynch offers a model for how congregations can collaborate with existing social service agencies to supplement their own ministries. Focusing on the distinct needs of prisoners, returning citizens, and their families, Dr. Lynch offers strategies for collaboration and suggestions for the types of partnerships necessary for holistic ministry.

The next two chapters highlight prisoner reentry and reintegration. In chapter 11, Rev. Lonnie McLeod focuses on the challenges involved in transitioning from prison to life "outside the walls." He calls on churches to recognize the significant trauma and adjustment involved in this shift. Dr. McLeod draws on both research and experience as a founder of the Exodus Transitional Community, a faith-based reentry ministry in New York that was designed by inmates as part of their studies at New York Theological Seminary's Sing Sing master's program. In chapter 12, Rev. Madeline McClenney-Sadler writes a letter to the saints, focusing on the role congregations can play in creating a welcoming environment for men and women returning from incarceration. Based on her research and work as executive director of the Exodus Foundation in Charlotte, North Carolina, she explains both a biblical basis for welcome and hospitality for the formerly incarcerated.

Chapters 13 and 14 address issues concerning the institution of the jail or prison itself and the nature of the local church's involvement there through chaplaincy programs. Chaplain Michael Smith of the Federal Bureau of Prisons focuses on the calling of the chaplain as an extension of the church. Smith's chapter includes an overview of the role of chaplains in state and federal correctional institutions, a portrait of the chaplain's role in relation to the rest of the correctional system, as well as to inmates and families, and a case for a firmer partnership between prison chaplains and local churches. Chaplain Elwood Gray follows up with chapter 14, drawing on his experience as both a local pastor and prison chaplain. His chapter concentrates on the key role prison chaplains play in working with families of inmates, and discusses how such work is enhanced when done in concert with local congregations. This chapter also considers opportunities for congregations to do volunteer ministry inside the prison system and in the local church beyond the basics of providing worship services and Bible studies.

Chapter 15 argues for a shift in congregational culture as a prerequisite for meaningful ministry to the incarcerated, returning citizens, and their families. Harold Dean Trulear reprises a number of issues discussed in earlier chapters, but with an emphasis on the question of how congregations can rethink their general approach to ministry by incorporating a focus on prison ministry and prisoner reintegration. The author poses again the question, "What if congregations treated incarceration as they do hospitalization?" In times of illness and even death, every congregation marshals its resources of care to individuals and families affected. What if our churches took the same kind of congregation-wide approach in responding to incarceration, rather than viewing prison ministry as the responsibility of a specialized, often marginalized, ministry team?

In the final chapter, Professor Lewis considers the role of public policy and advocacy in ministry to the incarcerated, returning citizens, and their families. He addresses (1) public policy and public perception as barriers to successful prisoner reentry and reintegration, (2) recent changes and opportunities within the realm of public policy that can enhance ministry, and (3) the church's mandate to become advocates for those affected by incarceration and not simply service providers.

The book's conclusion serves as both an afterword and a mandate. In it the editors push for ongoing conversation, dialogue, research, writing, and action concerning the challenges that crime and incarceration present to the African American community in this era. And they close with a call to the African American church to mobilize its resources on behalf of the true subjects of this book, all of whom are the objects of God's love.

A Church That Shows Up

The development and expansion of ministry to the incarcerated, returning citizens, and their families frame the challenge of this book. Each chapter deals with a specific dimension of this ministry, but all with an emphasis on relationship building, advocacy, and resisting the stigmatization that so often surrounds incarceration. We have assembled a team of contributors from a variety of backgrounds, all of whom hold in common a burden for those who have been imprisoned and their families. Some of us are pastors who minister in local churches. Some are social workers committed to justice and transformation for those on society's margins. The authors of this book include university professors, prison chaplains, and directors of social service agencies. Our numbers include a former mayor and one current congressional staff person. A number of us have personally experienced the difficulty of having a parent or family member incarcerated. And, at the risk of overemphasizing the "former" things, several of us have done time in state, county, and federal facilities. We have tried to be faithful in this text to the maxim "Don't talk about us without us."

What brings us all together is a strong conviction that the church has both an answer for those most affected by crime and incarceration and the resources to expand its witness in those arenas. There is nothing in this text that does not fit under the rubric of the gospel mandate. In building relationships with those on the margins, offering prophetic witness to a system that oppresses, and affirming that Jesus can and does change the lives of individuals and families, we simply bring to bear on those affected by the criminal justice system the very same faith and witness that have characterized the ministry of the church since Jesus said, "Go..."

When sin entered the garden, and humanity hid, God showed up in person. This book is all about helping the church show up today.

▪ NOTES ▪

1. The Annie E. Casey Foundation began its work in faith-based prisoner reentry in 2006 with the creation of the initiative Healing Communities. In 2010, the Casey Foundation turned Healing Communities over to the Philadelphia Leadership Foundation. This initiative calls for congregations to develop ministries to inmates, those returning from incarceration, and their families through developing networks of support within the congregation itself. Two handbooks, *Balancing Justice with Mercy* and *What Shall We Then Do?*, authored by Linda Mills, contain training information for pastors and laity. The handbooks contain the same ministry content, but with different theological orientations. *What Shall We Then Do?* was developed in conjunction with the Progressive National Baptist Convention Commission on Social Justice and Prison Ministry.

Commission members Rev. Owen Cardwell, Rev. DeeDee Coleman, and Rev. Virgil Woods assisted in its compilation. *Balancing Justice with Mercy* targets ecumenical and interfaith audiences and is used also with government and secular agencies. All are available on the Healing Communities website at www.healingcommunitiesusa.org. Also, see the Casey Foundation's report, *Healing Communities: A Framework for Congregations Ministering to Families Affected by Incarceration* (2010).

2. "Prison and Jail Inmates at Midyear 2008," Bureau of Justice Statistics, www.ojp.usdoj.gov/bjs/prisons.htm.

3. "One in 100: Behind Bars in America 2008," Pew Center on the States, February 2008.

4. Jody Sundt, Harry Dammer, Frances Cullen, "The Role of the Prison Chaplain in Rehabilitation," in *Religion, The Community and the Rehabilitation of Criminal Offenders*, edited by Thomas P. O'Connor and Nathaniel J. Pallone (New York: Routledge, 2003).

5. Lawrence Meir Friedman, *Crime and Punishment in American History*. (NY: Basic Books, 1994), 77–82.

6. Sundt, Dammer, and Cullen, "The Role of the Prison Chaplain in Rehabilitation," 62.

7. "Report of the ABA Justice Kennedy Commission Fact Sheet" American Bar Association, 2008.

8. This program offers a fully accredited master's of Professional Studies in Pastoral Care for inmates in the New York State correctional system. See Victoria Lee Erickson and Harold Dean Trulear, "Religion Class at Sing Sing Prison," in *New York Glory: Religions in the City*, edited by Tony Carnes and Anna Karpathakis (New York: New York University, 2001). Also, see the short story on this program aired by PBS at www.pbs.org/wnet/religionandethics/episodes/january-9-2009/sing-sing-seminary/1886/.

9. Lonnie McLeod, "Building a Reentry Ministry," presentation for Providence, Rhode Island, congregations March, 2008.

10. Hairston, Creasie Finney, *Kinship Care When Parents Are Incarcerated: What Know, What We Can Do*, Annie E. Casey Foundation (2009), provides an excellent and accessible overview to the issue with respect to children of the incarcerated and the resultant shifting of responsibilities and stressors of incarceration on the family. Prudence Zollinger's doctoral dissertation for the University of Louisville (2006), "The Needs of Children of Incarcerated Parents" approaches the subject in terms of the challenges and trauma facing these children. Another accessible report is "Families Left Behind: The Hidden Costs of Incarceration and Reentry," by Jeremy Travis, Elizabeth Cincotta McBride, and Amy Solomon (Urban Institute: 2003, revised 2005).

11. See the section on stigma and shame reduction in Linda Mills, *What shall We Then Do?* Progressive National Baptist Convention and Annie E. Casey Foundation (2008).

Chapter 1

The Stain of Incarceration

CHARLES E. LEWIS JR.

The disproportionate involvement of African Americans in the criminal justice system—particularly young black males—is arguably the single most pressing civil rights issue confronting the African American community. Many of the critical problems facing African Americans today—including concerns related to health, education, employment, family structure, and community development—are deeply connected to the fact that so many African Americans are involved with the criminal justice system.

In the past four decades, our nation has seen an unprecedented surge in the prison and jail populations. In the decades immediately prior to 1970, the number of people incarcerated in U.S. federal and state prison systems held steady around 200,000. Forty years later there are more than 2.3 million people housed in our nation's federal and state prisons and local jails on any given day.[1] Another 5.1 million individuals are currently on probation or parole.[2] The United States is now the world's leading custodian of the incarcerated, with an incarceration rate that is more than five times the world average.[3]

Although African Americans make up only about 13 percent of the total U.S. population, African Americans make up 37 percent of those currently incarcerated in the United States.[4] Even more striking is the percentage of African American men locked behind bars. Of the 920,000 African Americans in prisons and jails, about 850,000 are male, and fewer than 70,000 are women. So while African American men make up less than 7 percent of the overall U.S. population, they account for nearly 37 percent of people in prison and jail.

According to a report by Pew Charitable Trusts, one in nine black males between the ages of twenty and thirty-four is locked behind bars.[5] From 1974 to 2001 the number of black males who had been incarcerated at some point grew from 595,000 to 1,936,000. The number of black females who had experienced incarceration grew from 51,000 to 231,000 during the same period. In addition to those locked behind bars, another 1.1 million African Americans were under some form of community supervision (786,499 on probation and 304,866 on parole).[6] Unless incarceration rates decline significantly, about one-third of all African American males are expected to go to prison in their lifetime, compared to one in six Latino males and one in seventeen white males.[7]

How Incarceration Affects the Black Community

The record rates of incarceration among African Americans are intimately connected to a wide range of issues shaping our communities today.

HEALTH CONCERNS

Prisons and jails are incubators of infectious diseases that pose a danger to families and communities when inmates are released.[8] Every year a third of those in the U.S. population infected with hepatitis C, a quarter of Americans who are HIV positive, and 40 percent of people with tuberculosis go through the prison system.[9] Most often these infected people do not receive the medical treatment they need while incarcerated and do not have the resources to secure continuing treatment after they are released, posing a danger to other residents in the communities to which they return.

EDUCATION

It has been clearly established that poorly educated individuals are more likely to be incarcerated. Data available from a 1997 survey by the U.S. Bureau of Justice Statistics found that 44 percent of black inmates did not have a high school diploma or GED certificate, compared to 27 percent of white inmates.[10] In 1999 more than half (52 percent) of black men in their early thirties who were without a high school diploma had a prison record.[11] While most prisons offered educational programs, only 35 percent offered college courses.[12]

EMPLOYMENT

Given the low education levels among prison inmates, it is not surprising that incarceration is also closely associated with poor labor market outcomes.[13] A review of data from the Fragile Families Study concluded that fathers in that study who had been incarcerated earned 28 percent less annually than fathers who were never incarcerated.[14] Previously incarcerated fathers worked fewer weeks per year and fewer hours per week, and were more likely to depend on underground employment and off-the-book earnings.[15]

Devah Pager, an assistant professor of sociology at Princeton University, conducted a study designed to isolate the significance of both race and prison record in employment. He dispatched two cohorts of testers—one set of black testers and a set of white testers—to respond to employment opportunities in Milwaukee. Each group of testers was divided into two sets—one with criminal histories and one with no involvement in the criminal justice system. They were given fabricated resumes with similar education and work experience and randomly assigned to respond to employment openings.

Pager found that job seekers with a criminal history were half as likely to be called back by the employer, and white interviewees were twice as likely as black interviewees to be called back. But most disturbing was the fact that black interviewees *without* criminal histories were significantly less likely to be called back than white interviewees *with* criminal histories.[16]

FAMILY LIFE

If being incarcerated hurts an individual's earning capacity, it is possible that it may also have a negative affect on that person's likelihood to marry or form a stable family. However, it is difficult, if not impossible, to establish a definite causal link between incarceration and poor family formation, because other characteristics of those who get involved with the criminal justice system (such as poor education, limited employment options, and a history of risk-taking behavior) would make these individuals less desirable for marriage even if they had not been incarcerated. However, there is a growing body of evidence that black men are less likely to marry if they have been incarcerated.[17]

There is no question that the high incarceration rate of African American adults affects our children. In 2007, there were an estimated 767,400 African American children with at least one parent in state or federal prison.[18] As many as 7 million children have parents who are incarcerated or under some form of supervision on a given day.[19] It is reasonable to conclude that as many as 40 percent of these children are African American. Numerous studies have found that having incarcerated parents places children in greater risk for antisocial behavior and mental health problems.[20]

COMMUNITY HEALTH

The massive incarceration of blacks—particularly males—also impacts the political and economic health of our communities. Massive incarceration has robbed African Americans of a significant amount of political power. More than 1.4 million African American males have lost the right to vote because of felony convictions; this disenfranchisement rate means there are eleven states in which more than 10 percent of the African American population is ineligible to vote.[21]

The displacement of convicted individuals also creates large shifts in political and economic resources, as prisoners are often counted in the populations of the cities and towns where the prison is located rather than their communities of origin.[22] Inmates are included in redistricting counts, inflating the representation of elected officials in those counties. In some states, goods and services are apportioned based on population, shifting resources from the economically challenged communities prisoners leave to their new "residences" in distant communities.

When convicted individuals are assigned to serve sentences in prisons far from their home communities, ties to family, children, and social networks are disrupted. Costs to family members wishing to stay in contact are punitive, as visits to the prison may require hundreds of miles of travel. The U.S. Bureau of Justice Statistics reports that six out of ten incarcerated parents are placed in facilities at least one hundred miles from their children, with 10 percent serving time in facilities that are more than five hundred miles away.[23] In addition, telephone service providers place exorbitant surcharges on inmate-generated collect calls made from correctional facilities, which are passed on to family members. States often use these fees to recover the expenses of housing prisoners, yet it is family members, not inmates, who bear the costs.

Damages to families and communities are not always measurable in dollars and cents. Individuals and families are harmed by the breakdown of social organization in communities where crime flourishes. Some communities have lost as much as one-fifth of working age men to incarceration. As the Pager study revealed, those who manage to escape involvement with the criminal justice system are often stigmatized by the zip codes and neighborhoods they live in.

The Costs of Returning

Compounding the costs to families and communities of sending so many people to jail and prison are the costs associated with them coming home. Formerly incarcerated individuals more often than not return to communities that are economically challenged. Most lack the resources needed to make their transition successful. And more often than not they return home in worse shape than when they left.

Modern jails and prisons emphasize incapacitation and punishment—not rehabilitation. While the criminal justice system of earlier generations stressed the importance of rehabilitation, several research studies published during the 1970s led to skepticism about the effectiveness of rehabilitative programs and investing in inmate populations.[24] Prison education and work programs declined in the "get tough" political climate that followed. In 1979 educational staff accounted for 10 percent of all staff in state prison staff, and 41 percent of state prisoners participated in education programs. By 1995 educational specialists made up just 3 percent of the staff at state prisons, and only 22 percent of state prisoners were in education programs.[25]

Thus, most of those who are incarcerated—who were likely lacking in education and social skills when they were locked up—received little or no remedial assistance while in prison, and were contaminated by a criminal culture and an environment infested with infectious diseases. They arrived home in worse shape than when they left and now carry a stigma that will follow them for the rest of their lives. Most of them return to communities lacking the employment opportunities, affordable housing, and healthcare resources critical to their survival. Is it any surprise that two-thirds of the formerly incarcerated are rearrested within three years of returning home, and half of those rearrested return to prison?[26]

They are returning home in droves. In 2007, 751,593 individuals were released from state and federal prisons.[27] Only a small percentage of inmates are serving life sentences; approximately 95 percent of all current inmates will be released from prison at some point. As many as 10 million people are said to cycle in and out of jails in a given year, although there are no official data available.[28]

A Rite of Passage

Incarceration has become so much a part of the lives of young black males that there is an expectation of going to jail and prison. Incarceration has become a "rite of passage" in its own right and a badge of honor for many young African American men.

To use a baseball metaphor, special education and the juvenile justice system serve as the "minor leagues" for many young black males on their way to the big house. On any given day, nearly 100,000 adolescents are locked up in secure facilities across the United States, with many more in group homes and under the supervision of state and local juvenile justice systems. Statistics for 2006, the latest available year, listed 92,854 youth in residential facilities (78,911 males and 13,943 females); 1,200 were twelve years old or younger.[29] Although they represent just 16 percent of the general U.S. population in that age group, African American youth accounted for 37,337 (40 percent) of all confined youth, compared to 32,495 white youth (35 percent), and 19,027 Hispanic (20 percent). African American youth are overrepresented at every stage of the criminal justice process, making up 30 percent of court referrals and 58 percent of youth incarcerated in adult facilities.[30]

Prisons Are Big Business

Locking up lawbreakers—particularly young African American males—has become an industry. More than a decade ago, Eric Schlosser coined the term "prison-industrial complex" to describe the burgeoning system of policing, adjudicating, and incarcerating Americans, which he likened to the military-industrial complex that President Dwight D. Eisenhower warned about as he was leaving office.[31] Expenditures for corrections grew from $9.05 billion in 1982 to $68.7 billion in 2006, a 659 percent increase, or an average annual growth rate of 27 percent. When the costs for policing ($98.9 billion) and courts ($46.9) are included, the nation spent $215 billion on criminal justice functions in 2006.[32] As imposing as this figure appears, it does not account for the loss of human capital and economic productivity in GDP and income taxes.

Building and maintaining prisons has become big business in America. Rural towns are replacing industrial factories with human warehouses, swapping land and subsidized utilities for the jobs and other businesses that prisons provide.[33] The drive to build more and more prisons is spurred by the belief that there is a never-ending supply of law offenders to keep these institutions in business. Statistics over the past four decades supports this belief.

While the $215 billion spent annually on criminal justice functions is a concern for taxpayers who may lose other services to compensate for these costs, that money also supports the salaries and careers of hundreds of thousands of police officers, lawyers, judges, corrections officers, and criminal justice professionals. The California Correctional Peace Officers Association (CCPOA) outspends the state's teachers lobby association although it is only one-tenth its size—advocating largely for pro-incarceration policies.[34] Additionally, the private prison sector continues to grow with companies like the Corrections Corporation of America trading on Wall Street with a capitalization of $3.3 billion.[35]

One of the more egregious examples of profiteering from the prison-industrial complex was the conviction of two Pennsylvania judges for accepting $2.6 million in a kickback scheme to sentence youth to private juvenile facilities.[36] There are countless tragic stories about first-time low-level drug offenders receiving multiple digit sentences because of stupidity or naïveté.

What Can We Do?

What can African American churches do to stop the carnage? There has been a concerted effort on the part of federal, state, and local governments to involve churches and faith-based organizations in reentry strategies and other criminal justice programs. President George W. Bush made faith-based initiatives a centerpiece of his administration, and several significant church initiatives grew in response to that call. The National Alliance of Faith and Justice was founded as a partnership of community leaders and criminal justice professionals led by Addie Richburg, a lifelong criminal justice official and church leader. The Alliance focuses on promoting personal responsibility as a means to avoid engagement in the criminal justice system. Another initiative of note is the Prisoner Reentry Initiative of the Progressive National Baptist Convention, which seeks to promote healing in communities and help those leaving prison and jails reintegrate more effectively. Yet the question remains: "Are we doing enough?" Reviewing the evidence before us, the answer is clearly no.

Only when churches come together on a large scale to tackle the issue of mass incarceration will we see significant

change. While there are many different programs that address
the myriad of problems stemming from the overinvolvement
of African American males in the criminal justice system, almost all of them function independently. As noted criminolo-
gist Todd Clear observed, "While there are some quite active
prison-reform groups . . . there is no large and broad-based
citizen's group lobbying for prison reform."[37] He points out
that there are loud voices opposing prison reform in the form
of victims' rights groups and conservative political forces.
These voices, when joined with the enormous profits in the
prison industry, are a powerful force for criminal justice policies that prize retribution and warehousing over the rehabilitation, healing, and reintegration of returning citizens.

Historically, African American churches have led the fight
to triumph over oppressive societal challenges—from over-
coming slavery to overturning Jim Crow laws to creating
more equitable economic opportunities. Can African American churches galvanize around the issue of mass incarceration
and create alternative hopes and futures for African American youth—particularly our male youth? Our future depends
on finding a way.

▪ NOTES ▪

1. William J. Sabol, Heather C. West, and Matthew Cooper, "Prisoners in 2008" (Washington, DC: Bureau of Justice Statistics, 2009), 8,
http://bjs.ojp.usdoj.gov/content/pub/pdf/p08.pdf (accessed November 15,
2009).

2. Lauren E. Glaze and Thomas P. Bonzcar, "Probation and Parole in
the United States, 2008," (Washington, DC: Bureau of Justice Statistics,
2009), 1, http://bjs.ojp.usdoj.gov/content/pub/pdf/ppus08.pdf (accessed
January 18, 2010).

3. Roy Walmsley, "World Prison Population List," King's College London International Centre for Prison Studies, 1, http://www.kcl.ac.uk/depsta/
law/research/icps/downloads/wppl8th_41.pdf (accessed November 15,
2009).

4. Heather C. West and William J. Sabol, "Prison Inmates at Midyear
2008—Statistical Tables" (Washington, DC: Bureau of Justice Statistics,

2009), 17. http://www.ojp.usdoj.gov/bjs/pub/pdf/jim08st.pdf (accessed November 15, 2009).

5. Jenifer Warren, "One in 100: Americans Behind Bars in 2008" (Washington, DC: Pew Charitable Trusts, 2008), 34, http://www.pewcenteronthestates.org/uploadedFiles/8015PCTS_Prison08_FINAL_2-1-1_FORWEB.pdf (accessed December 8, 2009).

6. Thomas. P. Bonzcar, "Prevalence of Imprisonment in the U.S. Population, 1974–2001" (Washington, DC: Bureau of Justice Statistics, 2003), 4, http://bjs.ojp.usdoj.gov/content/pub/pdf/piusp01.pdf (accessed November 15, 2009).

7. Ibid., 1.

8. Prison Health Services, Inc., "New Parameters for Partnerships in Correctional Healthcare," 2008, http://www.prisonhealth.com/Whitepaper%20New%20Parameters_FINAL_05%2007%2008%20.pdf (accessed November 15, 2009).

9. Sarah E. Wakeman, Margaret E. McKinney, and Josiah D. Rich, "Filling the Gap: The Importance of Medicaid Continuity for Former Inmates," *Journal of General Internal Medicine* 24, no. 7 (2009): 860.

10. Caroline Wolf Harlow, "Education and Correctional Populations," (Washington, DC: Bureau of Justice Statistics, 2003), 6, http://bjs.ojp.usdoj.gov/content/pub/pdf/ecp.pdf (accessed December 8, 2009).

11. Bruce Western, Vincent Schiraldi, and Jason Zeidenberg, "Education & Incarceration" (Washington, DC: Justice Policy Institute, 2003), 6, http://www.justicepolicy.org/images/upload/03-08_REP_EducationIncarceration_AC-BB.pdf (accessed December 8, 2009).

12. James J. Stephan, "Census of State and Federal Correctional Facilities, 2005" (Washington, DC: Bureau of Justice Statistics, 2008), 5, http://bjs.ojp.usdoj.gov/content/pub/pdf/csfcf05.pdf (accessed December 8, 2009).

13. Bruce Western, Jeffrey R. Kling, and David. F. Weiman, "The Labor Market Consequences of Incarceration," *Crime & Delinquency* 47, no. 3 (July 2001): 424; and Charles E. Lewis Jr., Irwin Garfinkel, and Qin Gao, "Incarceration and Unwed Fathers in Fragile Families," *Journal of Sociology & Social Welfare* 36, no. 3 (2008): 77.

14. The Fragile Families and Child Wellbeing Study—a joint effort by Princeton University's Center for Research on Child Wellbeing (CRCW) and the Center for Health and Wellbeing, and Columbia University's Social Indicators Survey Center and the National Center for Children and Families (NCCF)—is tracking a cohort of children born in twenty large cities in the United States between 1998 and 2000. Additional information can be obtained at http://crcw.princeton.edu.

15. Lewis, Garfinkel, and Gao, "Incarceration and Unwed Fathers," 77.

16. Devah Pager, *Marked: Race, Crime, and Finding Work in an Era of Mass Incarceration* (Chicago: University of Chicago Press, 2007), 67–70.

17. Bruce Western, *Punishment and Inequality in America* (New York: Russell Sage Foundation, 2006), 144–46.

18. Lauren E. Glaze and Laura M. Maruschak, "Parents in Prison and Their Minor Children" (Washington, DC: Bureau of Justice Statistics, 2008), 2, http://bjs.ojp.usdoj.gov/content/pub/pdf/pptmc.pdf (accessed January 18, 2010).

19. Jessica Nickel, Crystal Garland and Leah Kane, "Children of Incarcerated Parents: An Action Plan for Federal Policymakers" (New York: Council of State Governments Justice Center, 2009), ix, http://www.nicic.org/Library/024054 (accessed January 18, 2010).

20. Joseph Murray, et al., "Effects of Parental Imprisonment on Child Antisocial Behavior and Mental Health: A Systematic Review," Campbell Systematic Reviews, 2009, 56, http://www.campbell collaboration.org/lib/download/683/ (accessed January 18, 2010).

21. Sentencing Project, *"Criminal Justice Primer: Policy Priorities for the 11th Congress"* (Washington, DC: Sentencing Project, 2009), 11, http://www.sentencingproject.org/doc/publications/cjprimer2009.pdf (accessed January 18, 2010).

22. Eric Lotke and Peter Wagner, "Prisoners of the Census: Electoral and Financial Consequences of Counting Prisoners Where They Go, Not Where They Come From," *Pace Law Review*, 2005: 587–88, http://www.prisonpolicy.org/reports/pace.pdf (accessed January 18, 2010).

23. Christopher J. Mumola, "Incarcerated Parents and Their Children" (Washington, DC: Bureau of Justice Statistics, 2000), 5, http://bjs.ojp.usdoj.gov/content/pub/pdf/iptc.pdf (accessed January 18, 2010).

24. Todd R. Clear, *Imprisoning Communities: How Mass Incarceration Makes Disadvantaged Neighborhoods Worse* (New York: Oxford University Press, 2007), 13, and Bruce Western, *Punishment and Inequality in America* (New York: Russell Sage Foundation, 2006), 173.

25. Western, *Punishment and Inequality* 175.

26. Patrick A. Langan and David J. Levin, "Recidivism of Prisoners in 1994" (Washington, DC: Bureau of Justice Statistics, 2002), 1, http://bjs.ojp.usdoj.gov/content/pub/pdf/rpr94.pdf (accessed January 26, 2010).

27. Heather C. West and William J. Sabol, "Prisoners in 2007" (Washington, DC: Bureau of Justice Statistics, 2008), 3, http://bjs.ojp.usdoj.gov/content/pub/pdf/p07.pdf (accessed January 26, 2010.

28. Nicholas Freudenberg, Jessie Daniels, Martha Crum, Tiffany Perkin, and Beth E. Richie, "Coming Home from Jail: The Social and Health Consequence of Community Reentry for Women, Male Adolescents, and Their Families and Communities," *American Journal of Public Health* 95, no. 10 (2005): 1725.

29. Melissa Sickmund, T. J. Sladky and Wei Kang, "Census of Juveniles in Residential Placement Databook" (Washington, DC: Office of Juvenile Justice Delinquency and Prevention, 2008), http://www.ojjdp.ncjrs.gov/ojstabb/cjrp/ (access December 5, 2009).

30. Alex R. Piquero, "Disproportionate Minority Contact," *The Future of Children*, 18, no. 2 (2008): 62–63, http://www.princeton.edu/

futureofchildren/publications/docs/18_02_FullJournal.pdf (accessed January 26, 2010).

31. Eric Schlosser, "The Prison-Industrial Complex," *The Atlantic Online*, December 1998, 3, http://www.theatlantic.com/doc/print/199812/prisons (accessed February 11, 2010).

32. Bureau of Justice Statistics, "Direct Expenditures by Criminal Justice Function, 1982–2006," http://bjs.ojp.usdoj.gov/content/glance/tables/exptyptab.cfm (accessed January 26, 2010).

33. Michael Welch and Fatiniyah Turner, "Private Corrections, Financial Infrastructure, and Transportation: The New Geo-Economy of Shipping Prisoners," *Social Justice* 34, no. 3–4 (2007–2008): 57, 60.

34. Alexander Volokh, "Privatization and the Law and Economics of Political Advocacy, *Stanford Law Review* 60, no. 4 (2008): 1221–22.

35. James M. Clash, "Jailhouse Stocks," *Forbes* 180, no. 4 (September 3, 2007).

36. Ian Urbina and Sean D. Hamill, "Judges Plead Guilty in Scheme to Jail Youths for Profit," *New York Times*, February 13, 2009, A0.

37. Clear, *Imprisoning Communities*, 11–12.

Chapter 2

Equipped for Effective Christian Correctional Ministry

KAREN SWANSON

The faith community has long been a part of correctional ministry. Christians answer Jesus' call in Matthew 25:34-45 by visiting the imprisoned, and upon prisoners' reentry, Christians continue this care by feeding the hungry, giving drink to the thirsty, inviting strangers in, and giving clothes to those in need. But the demand for correctional ministry continues to rise as the number of persons under corrections (including prison, jail, probation, and parole) in the United States increases (currently more than 7 million, or one of thirty-one adults).[1] The need for volunteer and congregationally supported correctional ministries is exacerbated as state budget crises lead to the elimination of paid chaplain positions and the early release of offenders in need of reentry services. These challenges create tremendous opportunities for the church and faith-based programs to step up and fill this correctional ministry void.

The question is: Are Christians prepared to meet the challenge? Many in correctional ministry can cite examples of times when well-meaning but ill-equipped Christians have done more harm than good in their attempts to minister to those involved in the criminal justice system. I believe one critical step in helping Christians meet these challenges effectively is to assure that both professionals and volunteers are educated and trained so their efforts at correctional ministry are helpful rather than harmful.

For the purpose of this chapter, Christian correctional ministry can be understood as reaching out to serve all those impacted by crime and its aftermath through the transforming message of the gospel and a holistic ministry grounded in love. This includes ministering to incarcerated persons and their families, formerly incarcerated persons and their families, victims and their families, and corrections staff.

The transforming power of the gospel provides the foundation for Christian correctional ministry: "So if anyone is in Christ, there is a new creation: everything old has passed away; see, everything has become new!" (2 Corinthians 5:17). Christians believe every person can be redeemed and transformed through the blood of Jesus Christ and the power of the Holy Spirit. We are called to fulfill our evangelistic mission by making Christ known: "This is right and acceptable in the sight of God our Savior, who desires everyone to be saved and to come to a knowledge of the truth" (1 Timothy 2:3-4). We are called to live and proclaim the gospel to all people no matter where they are spiritually. Scripture tells us Jesus had compassion on people and fed and healed them irrespective of where their hearts were in relationship to God. He told us the greatest commandment is, "You shall love the Lord your God with all your heart and with all your soul and with all your mind....And a second is like it: 'You shall love your neighbor as yourself" (Matthew 22:37-39). The apostle Paul reminds us, "So then, whenever we have opportunity, let us work for the good of all, and especially for those of the family of faith" (Galatians 6:10). These Scriptures provide biblical support for evangelistic and holistic Christian correctional ministry.

Christian Correctional Ministry Professionals and Volunteers

Few of the Christians now working within the correctional system as chaplains, case managers, or educators began their careers with a goal of serving behind bars. Most worked in other situations before finding employment in prisons or faith-based reentry programs. While these professionals may hold a bachelor's or master's degree, their formal schooling was designed to prepare them for work in a congregation, social agency, or school. Few received any preparation for the unique needs of working within the correctional system, either inside prisons or jails or among the formerly incarcerated. For example, the role of a corrections chaplain is different than that of a pastor. A typical master of divinity program requires few courses, if any, that address administrative duties, managing volunteers, working with those incarcerated, or providing counseling and services for those of other faiths, yet these tasks are the majority of a corrections chaplain's job.[2]

If professionals working in correctional ministry have received little training, most volunteers have received even less. A recent study by Tewksberry and Collins on prison chapel volunteers reported that most volunteers receive very little formal education or training to prepare them for their responsibilities in prison ministry programs. The authors note, "Though a majority of volunteers report that they are ordained, only one-third have university or seminary degrees; even fewer have been trained by a mentor or received instruction in an apprenticeship program."[3] While this study focused only on volunteers serving in correctional facilities, it is likely that volunteers serving in reentry ministry are similarly untrained for the challenges they face.

Nonetheless, most paid correctional ministries staff agree that volunteers provide a valuable service to the correctional institution, to persons incarcerated, and to those released from jails and prisons. Byron Johnson has noted the wide range of roles such volunteers play: "Faith-motivated volunteers in prisons are as likely to be involved in life-skills programs or instruction in GED programs as they are to conduct Bible studies or lead worship services. In this way, religious volunteers have played and continue to play a vital role in the vast majority of American correctional institutions. Indeed, besides work and educational or vocational training, religious activities attract more participants than any other type of personal enhancement program offered inside a prison."[4]

Each state has thousands of volunteers providing correctional ministry. Lennie Spitale writes, "It is a tribute to the power and love of God that he has sent—and continues to send—so many faithful volunteers to minister behind prison walls. The number of men and women has been so great and so all-encompassing that Christian volunteers have themselves become a recognizable part of the culture. Seasoned prisoners have come to accept these seemingly naïve, smiley-faced people as part of the common fabric of their prison experience."[5]

The critical importance of volunteers in correctional ministry only underscores the need for volunteers to receive training. Yet many such volunteers are reluctant to pursue such training, believing their prior ministry experience is adequate preparation for such work.[6] Time spent in training programs may be viewed as taking them away from "doing ministry" with little promise of value added to their effectiveness. Even those volunteers who see the need for training may question the need for any kind of higher education regarding correctional ministry, given they are not interested in pursuing correctional ministry as a career.

A High Calling

For many professionals and volunteers, then, the passion to serve in correctional ministry is strong, but there's a misconception that this passion and a Bible are all that's needed to minister effectively with those persons incarcerated or formerly incarcerated and their families. For certain, Christian correctional ministry requires persons called by God and devoted to making a difference in the lives of those impacted by crime and its aftermath; however, the high calling of the ministry necessitates both a passion to share Christ's love and education in the specific challenges of correctional ministry.

This creates the challenge of convincing both professionals and volunteers of the need for higher education courses in correctional ministry. Correctional ministry professionals may be thinking, "I have a degree; why do I need more education?" Volunteers may be thinking, "I have been a Christian and have volunteered for years. Taking courses is a waste of time and money when there are people in need and souls to be saved!" I believe the following story related by Duane Elmer will help address these concerns.

The Monkey and the Fish[7]

A typhoon had temporarily stranded a monkey on an island. In a secure, protected place, while waiting for the raging waters to recede, he spotted a fish swimming against the current. It seemed obvious to the monkey that the fish was struggling and in need of assistance. Being of kind heart, the monkey resolved to help the fish.

A tree precariously dangled over the very spot where the fish seemed to be struggling. At considerable risk to himself, the monkey moved far out on a limb, reached down and snatched the fish from the threatening waters. Immediately scurrying back to the safety of his shelter, he carefully laid the fish on dry ground. For a few moments the fish showed excitement but soon settled into a peaceful rest. Joy and satisfaction swelled inside the monkey. He had successfully helped another creature.

Reflecting on the story, Elmer points out;

> The monkey had good intentions and noble motives. He also had zeal. However, his motives were misdirected because of his ignorance—he could not see beyond his own frame of reference. He believed what was dangerous for him was dangerous for the fish. Therefore, what would be good for him would also be good for the fish—a crucial assumption. As a result, he acted out of his ignorance or limited frame of reference, and ended up doing damage rather than the good he intended. Unfortunately, the monkey may not even have known the damage he did, because he may have walked away leaving the fish "resting."[8]

Maybe you've experienced or seen situations where people were passionate about helping a formerly incarcerated person yet both parties ended up getting hurt. For example, one of the worst things a church can do is to put someone who's just come out of prison in the spotlight too early. Suppose a volunteer planning a men's prayer breakfast asks a man who has recently been released to share his testimony about accepting Christ as Savior while in prison. The former inmate is put into the spotlight too early, which places tremendous pressure on him to stay on the pedestal as he enjoys his newfound status. When he struggles with old or new temptations, he doesn't want to disappoint anyone, so rather than reaching out to the volunteer or other members of the congregation for help, he keeps silent and tries to deal with the challenges on his own. Without a supporting community, his silence results in failure and his return to jail. While the volunteer had good intentions, his actions actually contributed to the relapse of the inmate. Had the volunteer received formal education, he might have learned Lennie Spitale's "One-Year Rule," which encourages those reentering society to become involved with a local church but to stay out of the limelight for at least one year.[9] This rule gives newly released people time to adjust to life on the outside and develop stability.

Another way Christians serving in correctional ministry can do more harm than good is by operating with a "righting reflex" that tries to fix or make right anything that is wrong. We might think we are "rescuing" a formerly incarcerated person by setting his goals, making his plans, finding him a job, and getting him a car. But it would be far better to seek to help that person take responsibility for his own life by teaching him how to set goals, make plans, get a job, and find transportation. Another area where incarcerated persons are hurt is when professionals or volunteers preach what one former prisoner refers to as "beat-up" sermons—sermons that focus on how bad a person has been and how life can be different with Christ.

What Is Correctional Ministry Education?

So what kind of education is needed for effective correctional ministry? First, let me make a distinction between training and education. Training is often passive and generally focuses on learning a specific skill. Unfortunately, training may not have a lasting affect. How many workshops have you attended where you listened for a few hours and took some notes, only to go home, put the notebook on the shelf, and rarely, if ever, open it again? Training can be helpful in teaching certain skills, but there must be accountability for putting the learning into action. For example, mentor training may include empathetic listening with activities given to practice listening. But because there is no accountability beyond the training sessions, it is up to the student to continue to apply these skills to his or her ministry.

Unlike training, education is transformational learning—learning that requires a change in thinking and behavior. Effective education challenges students to examine their current perspectives and behaviors, engaging in critical reflection and discourse. This leads either to confirmation of existing beliefs and behavior or to adopting a new paradigm or perspective. It offers assignments that are designed to challenge students to go deeper in their understanding and holds them accountable for their learning. Effective higher education courses allow for praxis, a combination of theory and practice. The content taught is current, relevant, practical, and challenging. At its best, correctional ministry education weds information with experience, through assignments that require students to apply the learning in their current ministry setting and to provide opportunities for students to participate in collaborative learning environments and provide feedback. As transformational learning experiences, correctional ministry courses should include an integration of faith and learning, evidenced-based practices, and practical ministry applications.

Why Do We Need Correctional Ministry Education?

Why then should volunteers and paid correctional ministry professionals spend their time in courses designed to help improve their correctional ministry? I propose four reasons why both professionals and volunteers should seek formal education regarding correctional ministry.

1. TO GLORIFY GOD THROUGH THE PURSUIT OF EXCELLENCE.

Colossians 3:23-24 (NIV) states, "Whatever you do, work at it with all your heart as working for the Lord, not for men, since you know that you will receive an inheritance from the Lord as a reward. It is the Lord Christ you are serving." Working with all your heart includes the pursuit of excellence, which requires proper ministry preparation.

Jesus prepared for his own ministry through his time in the wilderness (Matthew 4:1-11), and he prepared his disciples before sending them out for ministry (Matthew 10:1-42). Missionaries going into a foreign country prepare by learning about the language, culture, and the land before beginning their ministry. Why would the expectations be any different for those serving in jails, prisons, or reentry ministries? This is especially important because most professionals and volunteers are unfamiliar with the culture, people, and environment. Educational courses that address the dynamics of working with persons incarcerated or formerly incarcerated, the criminal justice system, corrections, corrections staff, and spiritual formation are foundational to effective correctional ministry.

In addition, every one of the people you'll be serving in correctional ministry is created in the image of God and deserves your best efforts. These individuals may be marginalized by society but not by God. Remember to work with all your heart, for "it is the Lord Christ you are serving."

2. TO MOVE BEYOND THE LIMITS OF EXPERIENCE.

Experience is valuable and necessary for effective Christian correctional ministry. But our experience is limited to the circumstances and environments in which we've ministered and the people we've encountered there. Education provides a broader view, introducing a variety of resources, research, and ministry methods. Because there is a continual search to find "what works" in rehabilitation of offenders, education allows practitioners to stay current in the field of correctional ministry. Experience is important, but it is not sufficient. Education provides professionals and volunteers with the most recent ministry tools to help them improve their ministry effectiveness.

3. TO RAISE THE LEVEL OF PROFESSIONALISM

While the academic institutions and churches recognize the need for specialized education of their leaders, correctional ministry does not have the same level of professionalism. Although many Christian colleges and universities offer degrees or certificates in Bible, Christian education, youth ministry, worship arts, and even sports ministry, there is a dearth of correctional ministry courses, much less a major or certificate program. Certainly, professionals in correctional ministry who hold a bachelor's degree in education or a master of divinity degree have found the education they received in these programs vital to their work. Yet there is still a lack of content specifically addressing the unique needs and people served in Christian correctional ministry. Consider the words of Thomas Beckner, a pioneer in Christian correctional ministry education who founded the American Chaplaincy Training School (ACTS) twenty-five years ago: "For too long, correctional ministry has been a neglected area of study within Christian higher education, without an established core curriculum or a viable center of focused activity."[10]

One example of a college-accredited program is found at the School for Correctional Ministries, a program of the Institute for Prison Ministries at the Billy Graham Center, Wheaton College. The School for Correctional Ministries was formed through the collaborative efforts of the American Chaplaincy Training School, Christian Association for Prisoner Aftercare, Good News Jail & Prison Ministry, Prison Fellowship Ministries, and Wheaton College. These groups recognize and support the need for higher education in Christian correctional ministries. The school's Correctional Ministry credential program can be completed in one year and offers a combination of residential and online courses. It is available as an undergraduate or graduate program with an emphasis in correctional chaplaincy, reentry leadership, or a correctional ministry focus area. For more information, visit www.bgcprisonministries.com.

4. TO INCREASE THE CREDIBILITY OF CHRISTIAN CORRECTIONAL MINISTRIES AMONG NON-FAITH-BASED ORGANIZATIONS.

Government and community-based correctional agencies sometimes suggest that faith-based programs lack accountability, assessment, and evaluation. They contend that faith-based programs rely on anecdotal evidence as proof their work is effective. Yet such success stories are credible only if they represent the normative results of the program rather than a single shining exception. Correctional ministry courses provide religious groups with the education needed to properly assess and evaluate personnel and programs. It allows them to consider whether they have qualified staff and whether they are using a sound model that has proven to be effective and financially sustainable. It gives them the tools to do program evaluations that include staffing issues such as qualifications, ongoing training, and regular evaluations.

Faith-based organizations need to track and measure the success of their programs, publish their findings, and use data to inform program changes. Byron Johnson says, "Overstating program effectiveness without empirical evidence has often been a problem for religious volunteers and faith-based organizations. If their efforts are to be taken seriously, religious volunteers must understand that faith-based programs, like others, must be evaluated objectively."[11] Quality correctional ministry courses can help faith-based organizations gain credibility.

Let's raise the level of professionalism in the field of Christian correctional ministry, making sure we have the education and tools needed to do the job well. Then we can be sure that our efforts will bring glory to God and will provide quality care to those we serve.

▪ NOTES ▪

1. *One in 31: The Long Reach of American Corrections.* Public Safety Performance Project, The Pew Charitable Trusts (Washington, DC: March 2009).

2. Albert H. Votaw, "The Role of the Contemporary Prison Chaplain," *The Prison Journal* 78, no. 3 (1998): 282.

3. Richard Tewksbury and Sue Carter Collins, "Prison Chapel Volunteers," *Federal Probation* 69, no. 1 (2005): 29.

4. Byron Johnson, "The Faith Factor and Prisoner Reentry," *Interdisciplinary Journal of Research on Religion* 4, no. 5 (2008): 4.

5. Lennie Spitale, *Prison Ministry: Understanding Prison Culture Inside and Out* (Nashville: Broadman and Holman, 2002), 199.

6. Tewksbury and Collins, "Prison Chapel Volunteers," 29.

7. Duane Elmer, *Cross-cultural Connections* (Downers Grove, IL: InterVarsity, 2002), 14.

8. Ibid., 15–16

9. Spitale, *Prison Ministry*, 254.

10. Thomas Beckner, *School for Correctional Ministries* brochure (Institute for Prison Ministries, Billy Graham Center, Wheaton College, 2009).

11. Johnson, "Faith Factor and Prisoner Reentry," 14.

Chapter 3

Finding a Lazarus

KEITH REEVES

Remembering those in prison as if you were their fellow prisoners, and those who are mistreated as if you yourselves were suffering.—HEBREWS 13:3 (NIV)

...find a Lazarus somewhere, from our teeming prisons to the bleedign earth.—HISTORIAN TAYLOR BRANCH ON THE REV. DR. MARTIN LUTHER KING JR.'S "LAST WISH"[1]

On Sunday, November 15, 2009, in a rough, inner-city neighborhood of Chester, Pennsylvania (about fourteen miles southwest of Philadelphia), two young black males, ages seventeen and nineteen, engaged in a most incomprehensible act. Seeking to avenge a friend who had been shot in the eye, one of the two young men allegedly fired a gun in the direction of the violence-plagued William Penn public housing development. A stray bullet ripped through a brick wall and struck the head of Kathy Stewart, a devoted mother of three who was caring for her ailing eighty-five-year-old mother.

Police presumed the shooting was sparked by an ongoing feud between young men from the housing development and a neighborhood faction in the city's grim East End. According to the arrest affidavit and media reports, the two young men were laughing the next day about the shooting of Ms. Stewart. What's more, the affidavit indicates that the nineteen-year-old was dismissively blunt about his role: "They don't give a **** if one of our moms got shot, so I don't give a **** about her. . . . Yeah, we did that shit; we was chasing the bull on Franklin Street and hit the corner while we was shooting. . . . It is what it is."

We decry the senseless violence, even as we ponder the perennially urgent questions of "how" and "why" so many of our young black men could engage in such destructive behavior. Arguably, the path that leads to criminal activity—and inevitably to jail or prison—is set early for some. Chester, with a population of just 36,854, is a landscape fraught with despair, risks, and threats that often imperil young black males' opportunities. The statistics are staggering: an unemployment rate of 17 percent; 27 percent of the city's population living below the poverty line; 43 percent of the population under age twenty-four; and a sobering 32 percent of those age twenty-five and older who did not graduate high school. But equally unsettling is the brash tone and substance of the nineteen-year-old's remark—"It is what it is." For these words convey the blithe indifference, the sense of hopelessness and even rage of far too many young black males who are making life-altering mistakes and decisions against the backdrop of poor, drug-infested, inner-city neighborhoods across this country.

But in another sense, the words of the young man who fired the fatal shot that took Kathy Stewart's life hints at a deeper gulf—one that is more cultural and spiritual than anything else. Despite the fact that the percentage of black men graduating from college has nearly quadrupled since the passage of the 1964 Civil Rights Act,[2] or that the ranks of professional black men have swelled over the last four decades, or that household income for African Americans more generally has improved,[3] not to mention the historic election and swearing-in of the nation's first African American president, ever-increasing numbers of young males, disproportionately black, continue to swell the nation's jails and prisons. According to Harvard University sociologist Bruce Western, almost 60 percent of black male high school dropouts in their early thirties have spent time in prison.[4]

In Pennsylvania, Jeffrey Beard, the secretary of the Department of Corrections (now retired), has urged lawmakers to stem the growth of the state's prison population, which is bursting at the seams at 51,000 inmates, exceeding its capacity by 1,800.[5] Incredibly, the state's correctional system will expand by an additional 8,000 beds by 2013.[6] This is a chilling harbinger of not only the crisis to come—but also of the crisis already here. Indeed, the continued large-scale imprisonment of young black males (and, as this volume will also highlight, of young, low-income black women) threatens to overshadow and overwhelm all the strides African Americans have made since the days of Jim Crow and state-sanctioned racial segregation. And so we stand "at the corner of progress—and peril."[7]

This chapter seeks to accomplish several aims. First, I'll provide a broader, more nuanced, and extraordinarily telling portrait of young black males who are entangled in the criminal justice system. Second, based on my nearly seven years of experience mentoring incarcerated black males, I wish to present an explanation that challenges the prevailing wisdom regarding the reasons so many young black males are on a crime-prison trajectory in the first place. This alternative perspective will shed light on the views and behavior of those who often spend long stretches of time in and out of jail or prison. Finally, understanding that the experience of black male imprisonment is now almost commonplace in virtually every urban community, I'll conclude with a few pointed observations about what this disturbing trend portends for the relevance and cohesion of the contemporary African American church. With an estimated 50,000 black churches (including quite a number of wealthy, dynamic, and influential megachurches) and millions of congregants, there is reason to believe that black religious institutions can make a meaningful difference. The operative question is not so much what "the black church" will ultimately do or not do, but what role, exactly, it will play in raising the life trajectories of dispirited young black men and their families and children (the vast number of whom are left with deeper emotional and financial scars). Nothing less than the comprehensive and concerted engagement of the black church holds any promise of significant success.

Who Is in Prison—and Why?

The unparalleled and steady expansion of the U.S. prison population is a glaring symbol of something seriously run amok. As other writers in this volume have mentioned, the incarceration rate in the United States began to increase dramatically in the early 1970s. Incredibly, the incarceration rate today is nearly seven times what it was at the beginning of the twentieth century and experienced an almost threefold expansion between 1987 and 2007.

Providing explanation and context about the three decades of growth of people behind bars, Todd Clear, the author of *Imprisoning Communities*, has written:

> Back in 1970, when the prison population began to grow, nobody would have consciously chosen this future. But we have gotten here, surely and precisely, from making a generation of choices, starting about that time...during two lengthy periods of increasing crime rates, the prison population went up. But during the two periods of dropping crime rates, one in which we now find ourselves, prison populations also went up. That is, prison populations have increased during both economic downturns and economic recoveries. . . .

The most obvious consequence of unparalleled growth in the U.S. prison population is that it is now out of line, both historically and when compared with other nations.[8]

According to a widely publicized study by the Pew Center on the States and Public Safety Performance Project, "The U.S. is the global leader in the rate at which it incarcerates its citizenry."[9] That is, the United States imprisons more of its citizens than any other nation in the world—including South Africa, Iran, and China with its more than 1.3 billion people; and has a higher per capita incarceration rate than any other industrialized democracy.[10] At the start of 2008, more than 2.3 million adults in this country were behind bars, leading the Pew Report to conclude somberly: "Three decades of growth in America's prison population has quietly nudged the nation across a sobering threshold: for the first time, more than one in every 100 adults is now confined in an American jail or prison."[11]

Meanwhile, the mushrooming and upward prison trend "brought about both an absolute increase in the numbers as well as a disproportionately greater impact on persons of color,"[12] most particularly young black males. More than a fifth of all black men ages thirty-five to forty-four have been in prison—twice the percentage of Hispanic men and six times the percentage of white men in the same age group.[13] In fact, the Pew Center, having conducted an independent analysis of data from state and federal correctional agencies, calculated that 1 in 15 black men age eighteen and older was behind bars on June 30, 2006, as compared with 1 in 203 black women age eighteen and older.

There is one additional and important point to make about the scope and scale of these incarceration trends. That is, "the growth in imprisonment has been concentrated among poor, minority males who live in impoverished neighborhoods."[14] There is broad agreement, too, that the growth in the nation's incarceration trends that directly impact these urban neighborhoods is the direct result of a "wave of policy choices," including "the war on drugs," "three-strikes" measures, as well as sentencing policies and practices that kept lower-risk offenders in prison longer.

In the end, young black men in jail or prison constitute a fraternity all their own. And the troubling ramifications have been laid bare by social and policy analysts Peter Edelman, Harry Holzer, and Paul Offner who have argued that the impact of all this is easy to determine: "The effects of low incomes and high crime and incarceration rates are borne not only by the young men themselves, but also by their families and children, their communities, and the nation as a whole—which pays an enormous price to administer a massive prison system, and is also denied the productive labor of so many of its young men."[15]

Misguided Decision-Making on the Part of Young Black Males

How do we explain the grim statistics concerning unprecedented numbers of young black men in the bulging prison pipeline? Theories invariably include factors like: (1) the seeming intractable nature of inner-city poverty; (2) continued racial residential segregation and the attendant social isolation of those poor neighborhoods; (3) educational inequality and underperforming schools; (4) weakening family structure; (5) racism in the criminal justice system; (6) blighted and crime-ridden neighborhoods; (7) exogenous economic structures (i.e., the decline of manufacturing jobs, the suburbanization of employment, and the rise of a low-wage service sector); and (8) the lack of positive role models. Additionally, the suspicion of a causal relationship between the incarceration rates among black males and the destructive pressures and influences of the neighborhood and peer environment has been growing for some time as well. Clearly, the reality that an estimated 1-in-3 black men in their twenties is under correctional supervision or control is felt most acutely at the street and neighborhood level in urban communities. Importantly, this dynamic influences norms of social behavior and interaction, as well as the way in which young black males connect (or fail to connect) with the critical web of family, children, education, work, church, and authority (i.e., law enforcement and the courts).

In his deeply insightful book *Code of the Streets*, sociologist Elijah Anderson details the widening social isolation and disaffection of African-American males who reside in the poverty-stricken neighborhoods in inner-city Philadelphia. Anderson asserts that this isolation nurtures in these young black men an "oppositional culture" that is marked by alienation and "a certain contempt for a system they are sure has contempt for them."[16] Anderson's insights are supported by the research of Janelle Dance, who studied urban young people's attitudes toward traditional schooling. Dance finds that mainstream rejection "takes its toll with some students: it deflates and levels aspirations, creates a fertile ground for survivalistic, anti-mainstream sentiments, and renders individuals who are black...males, urban, and low-income more vulnerable to involvement in illicit street cultural activities." Professor Dance goes on to conclude: "During their middle and junior high school years, the vast majority of students in my study hold fast to their dreams despite this rejection. But as they mature into their late teens and early twenties, the constant mainstream rejection begins to weaken their resolve."[17]

Certainly, it is hard to refute the way in which these factors come together to limit the opportunities available to many young black men and to derail them in their pursuits. But based on my experience mentoring incarcerated black males during the last seven years, I suggest that there is something far more compelling going on: the penal crisis ensnarling young black men is rooted in misguided decisions on the part of the young men themselves. This alternative explanation—

that imprudent decision-making is a critical part of a complex puzzle of destructive community pressures—helps us get to the root of the problem.

In my years of conducting one-on-one mentoring with black men incarcerated for crimes they actually committed, the pattern was disturbingly common: growing up in single-parent households (not always female); coping with boredom; being exposed to values and behavior emphasizing toughness and a blatant disregard for authority; losing interest in school and eventually dropping out; selling drugs (and viewing it as an acceptable means of income and work); choosing the "wrong" friends; and, in the end, predictably being "at the wrong place at the wrong time" when something went awry. To be sure, poverty and cultural context play a key role in many cases. But the crisis is also one of values and behavior. In virtually every case, the incarcerated young black man whom I mentored had very damaged decision-making abilities. And in far too many instances, the erroneous decisions—often involving drugs and gun possession—proved catastrophic in the form of a lengthy prison sentence.

Dr. Milton "Mickey" Burglass, a former New Orleans inmate, contends that the central trait of those serving time is, in fact, the inability to make wise decisions. The majority of those who end up behind bars lack the skills required to set and prioritize goals and to carefully consider the immediate gains and risks as well as the long-term consequences of one's actions. In essence, they lack "the ability to think ahead, plan for the future, and repress impulses."[18] Burglass observes: "Most inmates live their lives simply reacting to what life throws at them...rather than stopping to choose how they would like their lives to be."[19] With this awareness, Burglass has established a targeted, motivational program (with curriculum) called Thresholds,[20] designed to teach incarcerated men six essential steps to decision-making. Through the use of a curriculum guide (or "workbook"), trained volunteers from the community teach inmates (or "clients") how to: (1) define situations, (2) set goals, (3) develop possibilities for reaching those goals, (4) evaluate these possibilities and explore the alternatives, (5) decide on a course of action, and (6) stay focused until one's goals are achieved.

In the Thresholds program, a volunteer from the community meets with a client once a week for a period of seven to ten weeks. Each meeting lasts one to two hours. During this time, the teacher and client cover the six steps outlined in the curriculum guide. Further reinforcement of the material is provided during group sessions, which are also held once a week. The group sessions include discussion, videos, and role-playing. Upon completing the program, each client is awarded a Certificate of Achievement. The program's central premise is that a person's image of himself/herself in relation to society strongly influences his/her actions. By learning to problem solve and make better decisions, clients raise their self-esteem, which enables them to be more productive upon returning to the community.

One mother who raised three children in the same Chester neighborhood where Kathy Stewart lost her life expressed her utter frustration this way: "Most kids get into trouble. But parents and mentors have to be there to help kids learn to make the right decisions." In fact, bad decisions need not be disabling. She continued: "Everyone is hopeless without goals. . . . The kids who are headed for trouble just want to make fast money. But you've gotta crawl before you can walk. It's a slow process to make a lot of money. But the end results [of working] are worth it. These kids just don't want to wait."[21]

The idea that the misguided decision-making of the young black males who are currently incarcerated contributes mightily to the bulging prison pipeline in this country is hardly astonishing. But it is troubling how much of our discourse avoids this fundamental fact. Too often we "miss the forest for the trees." And the tragic story of Kathy Stewart and the two young black men charged in her death is emblematic of how bad and impetuous decision-making sets in motion a chain of events that takes an incalculable and sorrowful toll on families and entire neighborhoods alike. And in this way, misguided decision-making is cause, correlate, and consequence for young black men living in impoverished neighborhoods. Even so, the poet Maya Angelou reminds us of something quite essential: "You may not control all the events that happen to you, but you can decide not to be reduced by them."[22]

Implications for the African American Church

Arguably, the African American church is uniquely equipped to deal with what criminal justice reform advocates have called "the collateral consequences of mass imprisonment."[23] And surprisingly or not, the church would likely find a receptive hearing. While the declining significance of religion in the United States is often lamented, according to a 2006 *Washington Post*–Kaiser Family Foundation–Harvard University national survey, some 81 percent of black men say that "living a religious life" is either "very important" or "somewhat important" to them. Among black men ages eighteen to twenty-nine, the percentage was even higher, with 87 percent agreeing with this value sentiment.

But addressing this need will require the black church to reexamine its assumptions regarding our often frayed and fraught relationship with young black men in prison, specifically, and inner-city communities, more generally. Economist Glenn Loury aptly describes why the church—with its prophetic voice—must act:

I once heard a twenty-two year old former gang member, who had had quite a few scuffles with the law, say, "You know, there's some stuff wrong with us only the Lord can fix." He was in church, trying to find his way back to a life of dignity and responsibility. . . . Fortunately, in every community there are agencies of moral and cultural development that seek to shape the ways in which individuals conceive of their duties to themselves, their obligations to each other, and their responsibilities before God. The family and church are primary among these. These institutions have too often broken down in the inner city, overwhelmed by forces from within and without....If these institutions are not restored, the behavioral problems of the ghetto will not be overcome. Such a restoration...must be led from within the communities in question, by the moral and political leaders of those communities. In the end, we are spiritual creatures, generations of meaning, beings who must not and cannot live by bread alone.[24]

The moral prestige of the black church is a resource and an asset such that the church ought to be a thriving and prominent institutional player in the restoration of the web of community, law enforcement, school, and government partnerships that once flourished in big cities.[25] Indeed, the breakdown of black families coupled with destructive community pressures mean we must demand more from the black religious institutions in our communities.

In the often-chaotic inner city of Chester, Pennsylvania, where more than 140 religious and faith-based institutions are sprawled across just 4.8 square miles, the gathering consensus is this: The ministry of the black church must reach beyond its provincial parishes and build a holistic ministry of caring—for ourselves; for our families, friends, and members; and for our communities. One of Chester's churches is the historic Calvary Baptist Church, where a young Rev. Martin Luther King Jr. preached and taught Sunday school while he was a student at nearby Crozer Theological Seminary. King lived in the Chester community for three years, and I have little doubt that he would be deeply troubled by the fact that many of our young black men in that city and others are "trapped in a trajectory that leads to marginalized lives, imprisonment, and premature death."[26]

In what historian Taylor Branch refers to as Dr. King's "last wish," the great preacher offered a profound challenge to us, urging everyone to "find a Lazarus somewhere, from our teeming prisons to the bleeding earth." The black church can help us recognize—and aid—the young black males in jails and prisons who are Lazaruses in need of our care. Only then can we begin the difficult but necessary task of helping them fashion a future for themselves, their families, and their children. As Branch argues, "That quest in common becomes the spark of social movements, and is therefore the engine of hope."[27] Suffice it to say that one prediction seems safe: hope will be a powerful determinant of whether the young black men returning from jail or prison are welcomed home by neighborhoods teetering on the brink of "chaos or community."

▪ NOTES ▪

1. Taylor Branch, "The Last Wish of Martin Luther King," *New York Times*, April 6, 2008, WK 15.

2. Staff of *The Washington Post, Being a Black Man: At the Corner of Progress and Peril* (New York: Public Affairs, 2007), 5.

3. The College Board Advocacy & Policy Center, "The Educational Crisis Facing Young Men of Color: Reflections on Four Days of Dialogue on the Educational Challenges of Minority Males" (January 2010), 7.

4. Bruce Western, *Punishment and Inequality in America*, (New York: Russell Sage, 2006).

5. *Delaware County Daily Times* (November 17, 2009), 12.

6. Ibid.

7. The line here is the subtitle of the text, The Staff of *The Washington Post, Being a Black Man: At the Corner of Progress and Peril*, (New York: Public Affairs, 2007).

8. Todd R. Clear, *Imprisoning Communities: How Mass Incarceration Makes Disadvantaged Neighborhoods Worse* (New York: Oxford University Press, 2007), 5.

9. Pew Center on the States and the Public Safety Performance Project, "One in 100: Behind Bars in America 2008" (Washington, DC: Pew Charitable Trusts), 5.

10. Joan Petersilia, *When Prisoners Come Home: Parole and Prisoner Reentry* (New York: Oxford University Press, 2003), 22.

11. Pew Center on the States and the Public Safety Performance Project, 3.

12. Meda Chesney-Lind and Marc Mauer, *Invisible Punishment: The Collateral Consequences of Mass Imprisonment* (New York: The New Press, 2002), 52–53.

13. *Washington Post, Being a Black Man,* 239.

14. Clear, *Imprisoning Communities,* 5.

15. Peter Edelman, Harry J. Holzer, and Paul Offner, *Reconnecting Disadvantaged Young Men* (Washington, DC: Urban Institute Press), 123.

16. Elijah Anderson, *Code of the Street: Decency, Violence, and the Moral Life of the Inner City* (New York: W.W. Norton, 1999), 113.

17. L. Janelle Dance, *Tough Fronts: The Impact of Street Culture on Schooling* (New York: Routledge Falmer, 2002), 5.

18. Jonah Lehrer, *How We Decide* (Boston: Houghton Mifflin Harcourt, 2009), 104.

19. Thresholds Teaching Manual, 7th ed. (2004).

20. I taught in the Thresholds of Delaware County program for several years and served on its board of directors for a year.

21. Personal communication, March 2005.

22. Maya Angelou, *A Letter to My Daughter* (New York: Random House, 2008), xii.

23. See, Mauer and Chesney-Lind, *Invisible Punishment.*

24. Glenn Loury, "The Spiritual Dimensions of a Societal Life," in E.J. Dionne Jr., Jean Bethe Elsthain, and Kayla M. Drogosz, eds., *One Electorate Under God?: A Dialogue on Religion & American Politics* (Washington, DC: Brookings Institution Press), 140–41, 143.

25. James Traub, "What No School Can Do," *New York Times Magazine* (January 16, 2000), http://www.nytimes.com/2000/01/16/magazine/what-no-school-can-do.html?scp=1&sq=Ja (accessed on March 5, 2010).

26. "America's Cradle to Prison Pipeline: A Report of the Children's Defense Fund" (Washington, DC, 2007), 4.

27. Branch, "Last Wish of Martin Luther King," WK 15.

Chapter 4

Theological Foundations for Family Connectivity

OWEN CARDWELL

Incarceration is never about a single individual. Incarceration is a family affair. When an inmate is *doing time*, an entire family is doing the time along with him or her. And the dramatic effect of a prison sentence on an entire family is particularly acute when the incarcerated person is a parent with young children.

According to the latest statistics from the U.S. Bureau of Justice, more than 1.7 million children in the United States have at least one incarcerated parent. State and federal prisons held an estimated 744,000 fathers and 66,000 mothers as of the summer of 2007. The majority of the incarcerated mothers were living with minor children prior to incarceration—including 64 percent of mothers in state prisons and 84 percent of mothers in federal prison. But this is not to say that children are not impacted by the incarceration of their fathers as well: 44 percent of fathers in state prisons and 55 percent of those in federal prison report that they'd lived with their minor children prior to incarceration.

According to the Service Network for Children of Inmates, parents in both state and federal prisons report having some form of limited contact or communication with their children during incarceration—including letters, phone calls, and personal visits. Mothers are more likely to have monthly contact with their children than fathers, yet only 54 percent had seen their children in the past year.

Children of inmates face a number of challenges. Statistically, those whose parents have been incarcerated are significantly more likely to find themselves incarcerated at some point. These children often experience feelings of isolation and embarrassment with regard to their parents' situations. These children have an increased potential for depression, lower grades, separation anxiety, impaired emotional development, acute traumatic stress reactions, survivor guilt, and delinquent juvenile behaviors, such as drug use, violence, and teen pregnancy.

Other articles in this volume have already shown the disproportionate numbers of African Americans involved in the criminal justice system. So it should not be surprising that African American families and children are particularly impacted by the incarceration. Is there a word from the Lord regarding our dilemma?

Family in the Bible

We begin by looking at a biblical understanding of the word *family*. The Old and New Testaments take slightly different approaches to defining *family*. The modern conception of a human family as consisting of father and mother in lifelong monogamy is alien to some parts of the Old Testament. According to *Harper's Bible Dictionary*, there are three Hebrew terms that have implications for an understanding of family: *bayit* (house), *bet ab* (father's house), and *mishpahah* (clan).

The smallest family unit was the nuclear family (*house*), which usually occupied its own dwelling. The house normally consisted of parents and their unmarried children, although occasionally nonkin, such as slaves or long-term visitors, also shared the family's living quarters. Within the household, the father held most of the authority, including legal control over his children and wife, although his power was not absolute (Exodus 21:7-11; Deuteronomy 21:15-21). Children were expected to honor and obey their parents; failure to do so was considered a serious matter (Exodus 20:12; Proverbs 30:17).[1]

The *father's house*, or extended family, was composed of two or more nuclear families that claimed descent from the same ancestor. In the Old Testament, the extended family acted as a corporate entity and was granted certain legal rights in order to maintain its solidarity. This understanding is very similar to the concept of extended family among African Americans today. We see the strength of the extended family played out in situations where another family member steps in to fill a critical role—such as an aunt or grandmother who acts as adoptive parent—often operating without proper legal documentation.

Several extended families were often linked together to form a *clan*. This Old Testament understanding has its parallels in the African American today, as many families extend their understanding of kinship to include second and third cousins as well as close friends.

The New Testament presents a view of family that is more akin to the Old Testament model of house (or nuclear family). As W. R. F. Browning writes: "The family in NT parlance consisted of parents, children, and servants (e.g., Matthew 10:25, 35; Romans 14:4) and the mutual relationships of all these parties are to reflect the kind of love which Christ has for his Church (Ephesians 5 and 6)....The performance and integrating of family life was in the interests of society and to that end the Christian Church...encouraged family life where security and shelter were provided and prayer and worship practiced." Browning goes on to point out that core teachings of the early church about family were adaptable to changing social conditions, and that this was, in fact, already happening within the New Testament itself.[2]

While the New Testament surely stressed the importance of relationships within one's nuclear and extended families, Paul Achtemeier has noted one critical added dimension in the concept of family as understood among the earliest Christians: "In the early church, support of one's family was seen as a virtue (1 Tim. 5:8), but the traditional view of family was transformed by seeing the Christian community as a new family (Galatians 6:10; Ephesians 2:19)."[3]

The African American church today has adopted a blend of the Old Testament extended family model and the New Testament family model. Our churches employ family terms of endearment within the church (Brother Jones, Sister Smith, Mother Harper, etc.). Yet the question for us, in line with Browning's insight above, is exactly how the core teachings about family that are found in the New Testament need to be adapted to our context today. More specifically, how can families (both biological families and the larger family that is the church) maintain connectivity when family members are incarcerated?

Key Biblical Concepts for Keeping Families Connected

The Bible is resplendent with the themes of redemption, forgiveness, reconciliation, and restoration. We tend to use these concepts somewhat interchangeably. However, I want to suggest that these four concepts represent a progression that, when applied to incarcerated families, suggests a process for maintaining connectivity.

A brief analysis of the definition of each term and an exploration of its biblical context might help make my point.[4]

Redemption can be defined as the act of buying or winning back; to redeem someone is to release that person from a debt or blame; or from the consequences of sin. The idea here is a transaction involving some type of payment that serves to release a person. The biblical root of the concept involves God's reestablishing a relationship with his people after acts of rebellion and sin have created a separation. The ultimate transaction is God's redeeming us through the death, burial, and resurrection of his Son, Jesus Christ. In response to what God has provided for each of us, we, in turn, are to extend the same grace to one another. This understanding of redemption can serve as a cornerstone upon which families can build connectivity throughout the course of incarceration and reintegrate upon the release of the family member from prison or jail.

Forgiveness is the act of giving up resentment of or claim to requital for; in other words, it is to grant relief from payment. Redemption makes forgiveness possible. In order for forgiveness to become actuated, however, repentance is a requisite. As members of the Christian community, our ability to forgive one another impacts community relations. When the family is able to forgive and lay aside the resentment sparked by the actions of the incarcerated family member, this paves the way for reconciliation and restoration.

Reconciliation is the act of restoring to friendship or harmony. When forgiveness is granted, relationships that were once broken and full of discord can be reconciled, and a sense of mutuality is reinstituted. This makes possible one final, closely related stage.

Restoration means to bring back or put back into a former or original state. While *reconciliation* and *restoration* can mean essentially the same thing, I would suggest that the implications of restoration are stronger and more far-reaching. While reconciliation involves return to a state of harmony, restoration is closely related to the theological concept of justification. In Sunday school, many of us learned a simple yet profound way of understanding what justification means: to say that I am *justified* means that things are *just-as-if-I'd* never sinned. In other words, the act of restoration or justification brings an offender back into his original status, just as if nothing had ever happened.

Two biblical stories involving families can help us gain a better understanding of how this progression toward restoration takes place. The first is the Old Testament story of Joseph and his family; the second is Jesus' parable of the prodigal son. While neither Joseph nor the prodigal son was separated from family because of incarceration (although Joseph was indeed imprisoned later), the point to be emphasized is the rupture that occurs in each family—and the process of healing that leads to restoration.

Genesis offers us the story of Joseph, a man sold into slavery by his brothers who were jealous of his close relationship with their father. Joseph had to endure not only separation from his family but also work as a servant in Potiphar's house, being accused of rape by Potiphar's wife, a subsequent imprisonment, and being forgotten by the pharaoh's cupbearer for two years after correctly interpreting a dream that resulted in the cupbearer's release from prison. However, eventually Joseph was asked to interpret a dream for the pharaoh. Not only was Joseph able to properly interpret that the dream foretold a severe food shortage, but he also suggested to Pharaoh a management system for handling the crisis. In response, Pharaoh elevated Joseph to second in command in Egypt.

When the famine forced Joseph's brothers to come to Egypt seeking to purchase food, they stood before Joseph but did not recognize him. Through an elaborate chain of events, Joseph eventually got his entire family relocated to Egypt, and in the doing so negotiated the process of redemption, forgiveness, reconciliation, and restoration among his family members. He eloquently tells his brothers that although they had intended their actions for evil, *God meant it for good*, to bring about a better future for them all (Genesis 50:20).

In Jesus' parable of the prodigal son (Luke 15:11-24), the younger of two sons demands his share of the family inheritance from his father. He leaves home and within a relatively short time spends all he has on cheap hookers and high-stakes gambling. When a famine hits the land, the prodigal is forced to hire himself out to a pig farmer. This act violates Jewish laws regarding ceremonial cleanliness and is indicative of how dire the situation is for this young man. Because of his severe hunger, the prodigal is just about ready to eat the corncobs in the pigs' slop when he remembers that the servants in his father's house have it much better than he does. He decides to return home and beg his father's forgiveness, even rehearsing his speech as he travels back home.

But the prodigal son doesn't get an opportunity to utter a word of his speech, because his father sees him "afar off," rushes to meet him, plants a kiss on his cheek, and places a robe on his back, a ring on his finger, and sandals on his feet. Additionally, the father orders his servants to prepare a welcome-home party, because his son who'd been thought dead is indeed alive. Again, we see the progression of redemption, forgiveness, reconciliation, and restoration.

In this suggested construct, each step of the process—from redemption to forgiveness, to reconciliation and restoration—requires just a little more effort and energy from the participating family members. Few families will be able to accomplish this monumental achievement on their own. This is where the church comes in.

The Church as Family

In recent years, we've seen a number of important efforts that point to the ways the church can support healing and wholeness for families whose lives are touched by incarceration. In 2008 the Progressive National Baptist Convention established a Commission on Social Justice and Prison Ministry, which is cochaired by Dr. James Perkins and Dr. DeeDee Coleman. With the support of a technical assistance grant by the Annie E. Casey Foundation, the commission published *What Shall We Then Do? A Family Freedom Kit for Creating Healing*

Communities. The stated purpose of the *Family Freedom Kit* is to help churches "minister to and disciple members of their own congregations who are affected by the criminal justice system—whether as defendants, prisoners, victims of crime or people coming home from prison, and the family members of all."[5] The *Healing Communities* model offers a framework by which the African American church can facilitate family connectivity.

A very practical example of how a church can facilitate family connectivity for incarcerated families is found in the Life Line Link project of New Canaan International Church in Richmond, Virginia, pastored by Dr. Owen Cardwell. Through a partnership agreement with the Virginia Department of Corrections, New Canaan provides videoconference visitation for families who have members incarcerated at Wallens Ridge State Prison (located 370 miles from Richmond). Since April 2006, New Canaan has connected nearly 2,000 family members with 650-plus inmates, at a fraction of what face-to-face visits in the prison facility would have cost. Recently the project has been expanded to include inmates at five additional prisons in Virginia, with additional visitor centers at the Shiloh Baptist Church in Alexandria and Norfolk United Methodist Church in Norfolk.

When it comes to the importance of strengthening families, the findings of a recent study released by The National Center on African American Marriages and Parenting are quite relevant. The study, which proposed to establish leading marriage indicators, found that in 2008 the percentage of African American children living with their own married parents was just 29 percent, and this number has been in steady decline since 1990. One suggested follow-up to this research would be a study of how incarceration in the African American community has factored into the destabilization of African American marriages and the number of children who are raised apart from one or both parents.

Linda Mills helps put the importance of this work in perspective:

> We care because it is our children, our families, our neighbors who are being arrested and imprisoned and are coming home from prison. We are talking about our families, our communities. . . . We care because it is our *mission* to care. Our work cannot stop inside the walls of our houses of worship. It cannot fail to reach out to the hearts and hearths of our neighbors. It cannot fail to reach inside prison walls.[6]

We in the church dare not leave those families who struggle with the sting of incarceration to try to make it on their own. Let us remember Paul's words, which call us to a broader understanding of family and to strive for reconciliation and restoration for all: "So then, whenever we have opportunity, let us work for the good of all, and especially for those of the family of faith" (Galatians 6:10).

▪ NOTES ▪

1. Paul J. Achtemeier, *Harper's Bible Dictionary*, 1st ed. (San Francisco: Harper & Row, 1985), S. 302.

2. W. R. F. Browning. "Family," in *A Dictionary of the Bible*, 1997, *Encyclopedia.com* (October 9, 2009). http://www.encyclopedia.com/doc/1O94-family.html.

3. Achtemeier, *Harper's Bible Dictionary*, S. 303.

4. All definitions are adapted from *Merriam-Webster's Collegiate Dictionary 11th ed.*, 2003.

5. Linda Mills, *What Shall We Then Do? A Family Freedom Kit for Creating Healing Communities* (Baltimore: Annie E. Casey Foundation, 2008).

6. Ibid.

Chapter 5

Amachi: Mentoring the Children of Prisoners

W. WILSON GOODE SR.

bout 10.7 million U.S. children ages eighteen and under have at least one parent who is under some form of supervision by the criminal justice system. More than 1.7 million of these children have a parent who is incarcerated in a federal or state prison or a local jail. The majority of children in these situations are very young: more than half are less than ten years old, and more than 20 percent are younger than age five.

Many of these children share the challenges faced by the larger population of this country's at-risk young people: including poverty, violence, limited opportunities for an adequate education, and a future that appears to hold very little promise. But children with a parent who is incarcerated or under supervision often face additional risks. In many cases, they have suffered the unique trauma of seeing a parent arrested and taken away. And with a parent's incarceration, their connection to a central adult in their lives has been cut off. While a parent is in prison, children might live with a grandparent, aunt or uncle, the other parent, or in a foster home or other facility. Some are separated from their siblings. Some are shifted from one caregiving arrangement to another. Often the caregivers are likely to be living in poverty and lacking the personal resources necessary to meet the children's needs.

Those needs can be complex. While research on the specific challenges faced by children of incarcerated parents is still in its early stages, studies suggest they suffer from a particular form of grief and loss that comes from having a parent who is alive but unreachable. The children may experience a complex mix of anger, sadness, shame, guilt, and depression. As a result, they often act out inappropriately and have classroom behavior difficulties and low academic performance. Not surprisingly, many of these youth end up in serious trouble themselves. In fact, according to a U.S. Senate report, children of prisoners are six times as likely as other children to be incarcerated at some point in their lives. Without effective intervention strategies, as many as 70 percent of these children will become involved with the criminal justice system. At one prison in Eastern Pennsylvania, men from three generations of the same family—a grandfather, his son, and his grandson—met for the very first time when they found themselves locked away in the same prison.[1]

The number of children at risk in these ways is certain to grow. The nation's prison population is increasing by almost 6 percent a year—and the number of women in prison is increasing even faster, having more than doubled since 1990. Since women are far more likely to have been a child's custodial parent before entering prison than men, the growing number of women in prison has led to even more children who have lost the central adult in their lives.

Despite their numbers and the intensified risks they face, these children have remained mostly invisible to policymakers, social service organizations, and sometimes even to their own communities. The Child Welfare League of

America has cited several factors that combine to hide them from view. Some factors are institutional: the criminal justice system has not traditionally been concerned with inmates' family relationships, and there is also a lack of communication between prisons and child welfare agencies. Other factors are a result of deeply ingrained personal feelings: children and other relatives feel shame about incarcerated family members and fear being stigmatized. Thus, they tend to remain silent and reluctant to ask for assistance. Therefore, mentoring organizations must use external sources such as visitations to prisons to help identify children placed at risk by the incarceration of a parent.

In 1999, with generous funding from the Pew Charitable Trusts, Public/Private Ventures (P/PV) a national nonprofit organization that seeks to improve the effectiveness of social policies and programs, began developing a mentoring program for children of incarcerated and formerly incarcerated parents in Philadelphia. This mentoring program would later be replicated nationwide. The initiative was named Amachi—a West African word that means "who knows but what God has brought us through this child." Volunteers would be recruited from city congregations to provide one-to-one mentoring to the children. And beyond being a primary source of mentors, local congregations would be key partners in the initiative.

There were several reasons the Amachi program sought significant involvement from churches. In the communities where the mentored children live, the church is often the most important remaining institution. Local congregations have long been a valued source of volunteers who are forces for positive change. Church volunteers help feed the hungry and provide shelter for the homeless. They run daycare centers, build housing for senior citizens, and operate after-school programs. Thus, it was logical to believe congregations that see their missions as extending beyond the walls of their buildings and into their communities would respond to

Amachi's vision of providing crucial support for children in their neighborhoods.

Why Mentoring?

Because children of incarcerated parents have not, until recently, been recognized as a specific group with special needs, there is little knowledge about what interventions might measurably improve their prospects in life. But what is known is that, in many cases, these children are attempting to grow up without a steady, reliable adult in their lives. And there's no question that a consistent, nurturing relationship with a dependable adult is an essential developmental support for children.

Evidence has shown that mentors can make a tangible difference in young people's lives. In the mid-1990s, P/PV conducted a study of the work of the nationally known mentoring organization, Big Brothers Big Sisters of America (BBBSA). The results showed that having a mentor—a consistently caring and supportive adult—significantly reduced a young person's initiation of drug and alcohol use, improved school performance and attendance, and reduced incidences of violence. Given these realities, mentoring would seem to be a promising approach for responding to the challenges facing children with an incarcerated parent.

Amachi adopted the motto, "People of Faith Mentoring Children of Promise." And the project—a partnership of P/PV, BBBSA, and the Center for Research on Religion and Urban Civil Society (CRRUCS) at the University of Pennsylvania—got up and running at a rapid pace. It began recruiting churches in November 2000; by April 2001 the first mentors were meeting with youth. By the end of January 2002, Amachi was already operating in 42 churches and had made almost 400 matches throughout Philadelphia.

The Amachi program's innovative design includes three key elements:

1. *The support and involvement of faith-based con-gregations from the youngsters' own or nearby neighborhoods.* Drawing on a sense of compassion and spiritual mission, these congregations provide the volunteer mentors for the Amachi program.

2. *The promotion of strong personal relationships be-tween youth and their mentors.* Following the one-to-one community-based model widely implemented by Big Brothers Big Sisters, Amachi pairs children and adults in mentoring relationships that require frequent and regular contact between the adult mentor and the child. These relationships last up to a year—and some-times longer.

3. *Professional case management and support for each pairing to help ensure that the child, his or her family, and the mentor can all work together harmoniously.* The model brings a secular organization with adminis-trative and management acumen (usually Big Brothers Big Sisters) to partner with members of local congre-gations to mentor children of inmates.

Of course, the heart of this approach is matching each child with a loving and caring adult. Research shows that if a loving and caring adult spends at least one hour once per week with a child in a mentoring relationship (or at least two hours twice per month), that child is more likely to achieve success. Local congregations provide the volunteer mentors, and the secular agency provides administrative infrastructure to investigate the backgrounds of volunteers, conduct interviews, provide training, do the matching, and supply mentor support.

Spreading the Mentoring Message

Amachi's impact has also reached beyond the congregations and the children who are directly involved. The program's start-up in Philadelphia coincided with President George W. Bush's stated policy goal of stimulating faith-based initiatives as a means of addressing many social ills, drawing on the unique blend of traditional community presence and compassion found in congregations across the United States. In his 2003 State of the Union Address, the President specifically proposed a $150 million initiative that would bring mentors to 100,000 children of prisoners. This led the federal Family and Youth Services Bureau (FYSB) to create a Mentoring Children of Prisoners (MCP) program, which supports some 220 such efforts nationally.

Such large-scale public policy efforts provide resources—and thus the impetus for local programs to meet some of those needs swiftly. And there is hope that they may stimulate more sustained programmatic attention and support for these children. Yet the risk is that local organizations, unaware of the many challenges and intricacies of programs like Amachi, may look to start new programs without the necessary tools and knowledge to make these programs effective. The rush to implement, spurred by the national visibility and the availability of federal funding, may prove wasteful, unhelpful, and even discouraging to the children it seeks to assist unless it is tempered by sound planning and attention to program design and operation. In September 2010 the FYSB awarded $36.8 million in MCP funding to 95 grantees nationwide. Since 2003 the FYSB has awarded $129.5 million to more than 220 grantees.

And that is the challenge: to sustain the visibility and momentum of such initiatives while also ensuring that new programs everywhere benefit from the lessons learned and best practices already achieved—meaning they have clear goals, are solidly planned and implemented, and have adequate resources and effective staff and management. The Amachi experience proves that, while the basic concept is straightforward, implementation is not. There needs to be a careful sequence of recruiting the collaborative partners essential to the program's success; reaching out effectively to faith leaders and congregations; creating relationships with prisons and prisoners; and establishing a balance between the natural compassion to be found in faith congregations and the professional practices, standards, and management that effective programs require.

It was for that reason that the Amachi Training Institute was established to build the capacity of mentoring organizations on a broad scale. Each Amachi program begins with a day and a half of training, followed by technical assistance to help programs recruit volunteers and identify children via their parents in local prisons. This hands-on partnership puts the training into action. All programs also receive training on the appropriate use of government funds.

Amachi has conducted 141 Amachi training courses for 3,536 people from 1,026 organizations in 559 cities in forty-seven states, as well as Canada, Puerto Rico, and the District of Columbia. In addition, Amachi conducted 268 site visits, providing technical assistance to 226 agencies in 116 cities in forty-two states and the District of Columbia, resulting in rapid program replication and growth. Since 2001 more than 250,000 children have been served by the 359 agencies in this program.

Recent and ongoing studies of the Amachi model in the state of Texas report that 97.6 percent of children participating in Amachi programs are promoted to the next grade level, 78.7 percent of adults report an improvement in child self-confidence, 52 percent of children are less likely to skip school, and 47.7 percent of children report better academic performance. Through the second year of this three-year longitudinal study, not one of the Amachi youth had been referred to the juvenile justice system.[2]

In the fall of 2009, Amachi received a three-year $17 million grant from the Office of Juvenile Justice and Delinquency Prevention to operate the Amachi Mentoring Coalition Project designed to provide financial resources, training, and technical assistance to mentoring organizations nationwide that serve children impacted by incarceration. As of October 2010, through this program 5,648 children were matched with a mentor, 128 jobs were created, 399 partnerships were formed, and eight statewide coalitions were created. It is intended that by June 2012, there will be thirty-eight statewide coalitions across the nation working on behalf of children impacted by incarceration.

Programs like Amachi that aim to assist young people through mentoring have clearly proven to be effective. Stable mentoring relationships have been shown to reduce risky behavior and promote achievement among disadvantaged youth, and there is hope that such efforts will reduce the number of children who follow their parents to jail. While we must surely work to improve the effectiveness of reentry programs for those rejoining our communities after being released from our prisons and jails, it is clear that "no entry" programs are far more effective. Mentoring programs like Amachi aim to slowly dismantle the prison-industrial complex by helping children of the incarcerated avoid repeating the mistakes that led their parents to prison, thereby making the growth in prison construction and reentry programs unnecessary. It will also take legislative and policy changes to rescind laws enacted in the 1990s. These laws requiring mandatory maximum and minimum sentencing are largely responsible for the dramatic increase in incarceration over the last two decades. It is my belief that these policies and legislative changes along with mentoring of the children could cut the prison population 50 percent by 2020.

▪ NOTE ▪

1. Some information contained in this chapter is also referred to in two other publications of PPV: Linda Jacovy's *Amachi: Mentoring children of prisoners in Philadelphia* (2003); and W. Wilson Goode Sr. and Thomas J. Smith's *Building from the Ground up* (2005).

2. Year two results of a three-year longitudinal study of Amachi Texas, funded through the Office of Juvenile Justice and Delinquency Prevention.

Chapter 6

Breaking the Chain: Partnerships for Ministry to Children of Prisoners

DEBORAH JACKSON-MEYERS

"It is not the will of your Father in heaven that one of these little ones should be lost."—MATTHEW 18:14

The relationship between the criminal behavior patterns of parents and caretakers and the behavior of youth is widely recognized. Popular literature, journal articles, clinical writings, social work case studies, and police reports all reveal a correlation between certain family situations and the deviant behaviors of young people. Although there has been very little systematic study of inter-generational transmission of criminal behaviors, there is no question the children of parents with a criminal history are more likely to find themselves behind bars.

We in the African American faith community are losing a disproportionate number of our youth to delinquency, gangs, violence, drugs, sexual diseases, and homicide. In the face of this reality, we can no longer do ministry as usual. We cannot say, "Give me that old time religion, it's good enough for me," because it is not good enough. To save the children and youth of the very neighborhoods in which our congregations are located, the church is compelled to respond to the problem of African American intergenerational criminal patterns.

The Breaking the Chain Foundation (BTC) seeks to meet the spiritual, emotional, educational, and psychological needs of children and youth affected by the chains of intergenerational incarceration. We have developed a model designed to provide a wide range of services to children and youth whose parent(s) are incarcerated or under correctional supervision. We seek out and employ biblical principles that will inform, assist, and empower the children, youth, and families affected by incarceration. Through advocacy, crime prevention, and intervention efforts, we minister holistically and systematically in ways that will reduce, and ultimately eradicate, intergenerational incarceration.

Ending the Cycle

Criminal behavior among juveniles in the African American community is often linked to the behavior of the generations before them—the criminal activity of their parents, grandparents, and caretakers. Parents are a child's primary source of learning—so when parents display deviant behaviors, their children are likely to adopt similar kinds of behavior. According to Frederick Elkin, author of *The Child and Society: The Process of Socialization*, children adopt some behavior patterns that are unique to their particular families and others that are characteristic of the larger culture.[1] Despite the fact that many children never intend to choose a life of crime, they are often drawn into such a life as a result of negative family influences, behaviors, and lifestyles.

Furthermore, the criminal activity of each succeeding generation tends to be more violent. Our youth are contending with hard-core problems and facing critical behavioral decisions at an age when they are terribly vulnerable to outside pressures. Most young adolescents seem to be lacking a clear sense of themselves and end up searching for identity via trial and error. A. Comer and J. Poissant have written: "We have seen failure, criminal behavior, extreme militant behavior, depression, and even outright mental breakdown result from such identity confusion. . . . African American adolescents in particular may succumb to despair, and many give up."[2]

Traditionally, the style of child rearing in the African American tradition emphasizes religious beliefs, strict discipline, respect for parental authority, and reliance on experience as the teacher. This approach has been handed down through the generations—from grandparent to parent to child. Strength, perseverance, hope, and faith are among the most important values elders have sought to pass on through the generations.[3] Over the years the passing down of these values and cultural expectations has been sustained by the proximity of young to the old.

More recently, however, socioeconomic and political stressors of society have complicated the ability of the extended units to remain in intimate contact. As a consequence, the character development of younger generations has been severely impaired, particularly around values pertaining to religion, discipline, education, work, sex, marriage, mutual aid, race identity, and death.[4] The incarceration of one or more parents only increases the severity of this breakdown for many youth.

The Breaking the Chain model is rooted in the belief that children and youth who are exposed to powerful positive influences early in life and taught empowering tools will be able to break the cycle of intergenerational deviant behaviors that too often leads to incarceration. Youth whose parents have made poor decisions must transcend this environmental pollution in order to achieve a holistic development of mind, body, and spirit as a part of their everyday lives. We seek to provide youth with the resources and influences that can guide them toward making those positive choices.

We are losing a large percentage of this generation because the church has not developed ministries or collaborated with community agencies that speak specifically to the problem of intergenerational criminal patterns of behavior. Addressing the special needs of the children and families of the incarcerated requires the partnership of the entire community: teachers, community service providers, social workers, health care providers, community activists, political leaders, members of religious communities, and all others who have an interest in the well-being of children. We must begin working together across disciplines, systems, and cultures to create a web of support for children and families involved with the criminal justice system and separated by incarceration. If communities come together to meet their needs, better outcomes are possible.[5]

With that in mind, our model encourages churches to collaborate with community leaders and governmental agencies in a dialogue that will begin focusing on the root of the problem in order to break the ongoing cycle of intergenerational patterns of criminal behavior among juveniles.

We advocate an approach we call Prescribe Preventive Ministry/Services (PPM/S), which seeks to identify and respond to the root causes of their local juvenile delinquency problems through comprehensive, collaborative prevention planning. Too often the church creates programs and ministries that seek to put a Band-Aid over the problem rather than addressing its root causes. We must identify the root causes of juvenile crime and implement a range of preventive programs that are ministerial in nature and nurturing to prevent delinquency from occurring in the first place. When offenses occur, churches must become proactive and advocate along with other community agencies to defuse and control the conduct at the earliest opportunity. By attacking the problem of juvenile delinquency and crime from the perspectives of public safety, accountability, and care and concern for every child—through both prevention and delinquency control—we can achieve the greatest success in enhancing positive youth development and reducing juvenile crime.[6]

When looking to the root causes of crime, scholars have noted the affects of poverty and segregation on the black family and youth in particular. The lack of educational opportunities and other resources often propel the child into a life of criminal or deviant behavior. The majority of black youth are still at risk in public schools that are often de facto segregated, with unemployment, drugs, teenage pregnancy, and dropping out remaining serious problems.[7] The impact of incarceration is another variable that causes a family to become "at risk."

For the most part, the needs of the families of both prisoners and returning offenders are neglected throughout the whole of the criminal justice process—from arrest to arraignment to trial to placement in a correctional facility to reentry. In addition, these families often fall through the gaps in social services because agencies are not aware of their special needs, or because there are no programs to meet those needs.[8]

Recognizing this, it is of great importance for the church, and particularly the African American church, to become more of an effective agent in responding to this epidemic of intergenerational incarceration affecting children and youth. The African American church cannot ignore its responsibility when it has the ability to provide significant resources needed by the community. If African American ministers are to make the gospel message real in the lives of African American people, they must respond to the reentry call and the urgent concerns of the families involved.

The Breaking the Chain Model

Our approach is designed to intervene in the cycle of criminal behavior and intergenerational incarceration by addressing the causes of such behavior, while also providing services to children and families at risk and affected by incarceration. We do this in the following ways:

- Identify churches with active and vibrant prison ministry programs for youth, adults, and families.
- Develop partnerships with juvenile homes, detention centers, and other agencies that will assist in the development of children and youth impacted by incarceration.
- Build relationships with community organizations that can help identify families with a history of incarceration so we can link these families to faith-based organizations.
- Offer a comprehensive prevention and intervention program for youth that is designed to reduce crime by addressing its root causes.
- Establish and implement a case management tool that is tailored to meet the specific needs of children.

Specifically, the Breaking the Chain model seeks to serve youth through four key programs:

1. *Mentoring Program:* We link youth between the ages of ten and seventeen with caring adult mentors for the purpose of gaining necessary support to navigate through difficult circumstances. Adults assist youth in a variety of ways, helping them make positive life choices, enhance their commitment to academic success, and build ambition toward achieving their personal goals.
2. *Sponsoring Program:* We also connect youth between the ages of six and seventeen with caring adult sponsors who can offer economic support to assist monetarily these children through difficult circumstances.
3. *Tutoring Program:* We provide volunteer tutors or homework centers in area churches to help build reading and math skills. These tutors are a resource not

only to the youth with whom they are linked, but also to adult offenders transitioning back into the larger society.

4. *Referral Program:* After administering a baseline assessment of each individual youth and his or her needs, we make referrals to specialized providers who can render professional services to youth who may need psychological counseling, academic support, nutritional services, pastoral care and counseling, and recreational programs.

Ministers, teachers, counselors, and other community leaders can provide the important and necessary resources for youth in helping them to establish meaningful bonds with church, school and the community. Cultural values can be incorporated into ministries, programs, and curricula to help youth better understand and appreciate their heritage, which can, in turn, foster a sense of self-worth. We can help youth identify their strengths and talents, and thus strengthen their resiliency. Recognition of their knowledge, talents, and skills can make a difference with youth who are affected by incarceration and live in chaotic and dangerous places.

Churches are central to this process within African American communities. The black church is a visible fellowship, an institution with great economic, social, and political influence. It is the only massive organization owned and controlled by black people in a white racist society. But it is, at the same time, an invisible fellowship, an organism of the Spirit. It is the household of faith, the family of God. In its nature and mission, it can minister to the whole person—to head, heart, and stomach. No other institution in the black community can make that statement.[9] It is important that we maintain this sense of togetherness, belonging, human pride, self-respect, dignity, mutual love, and concern. What we call the family spirit must permeate our Christian fellowship of black people. Beyond this we must cultivate a black ecumenism that will establish a unity among black Christians as they affirm their personhood in Christ, which is denied them in society.

If we can heal the brokenness in family life, we will be on the way to unity, power, and love among ourselves that will deal a powerful blow to structures of power that perpetuate injustice against our people. As a people of God, as the household of faith, as the family of God, the black church must uphold by word and deed the ideal pattern of family life to the youth of our communities. In worship, service, and action, the "family" must be the model of all relationships both human and divine, to the end that the black family may be a part of the black church and the black church may be an extension of the black family, to the end that God may be "the Father, from whom every family in heaven and on earth is named."[10]

■ NOTES ■

1. F. Elkin, *The Child and Society: The Process of Socialization* (New York: Random House, 1968), 47–49.

2. J. Comer and A. Poissant, *Raising Black Children* (New York: Penguin, 1992), 299.

3. M. A. Orlandi, *Cultural Competence for Evaluators: A Guide for Alcohol and Other Drug Abuse Prevention Practices Working with Ethnic Racial Communities* (Rockville, MD: DHHS Publication, 1992), 45–46.

4. Orlandi, *Cultural Competence*, 46.

5. C. Seymour, *Childwelfare League of America: What Can You Do to Help?* www.cseymour.com.

6. H. Snyder, *Juvenile Arrests 1998 Report* (Washington, DC: Office of Juvenile Justice and Delinquency, 1999).

7. H. P. McAdoo and J. L. McAdoo, *Black Children: Social, Educational and Parental Environments* (Beverly Hills: Sage, 1985), 77–79.

8. E. Hostetter and D. Jinnah, *Families of Adult Prisoners* (Prison Fellowship Ministries, 1993) http://www.fcnetwork.org/reading/researc.html.

9. Harrell B. Roberts, *The Inner World of the Black Juvenile Delinquent: Three Case Studies* (Hillsdale: NJ Lawrence Erlbaum Associates, 1987), 35.

10. Ibid., 36.

Chapter 7

Nurturing a "Woman Kind of Faith": Ministry to Women in Incarceration and Reentry

ALFREDA ROBINSON-DAWKINS

lthough the dominant image of incarceration in the African American community is of black men, black women cannot be forgotten. In fact, African American women constitute the fastest-growing population in our state and federal prisons. This chapter deals squarely with the issue of female incarceration, including its connection to male-female relationships, how women make choices, and how congregations can be part of the support system women need both during incarceration and in the transition back to home, community, and society.

I view these issues through the lens of my own experience. My work with the National Women's Prison Project, especially as we attempt to assist congregations in their efforts to work with women in general and African American women in particular, flows directly from my own personal testimony, which begins with my own cry of anguish: "Why Lord? Why? Why did I have to go to prison?"

I asked God that question many times during my 121-month federal sentence spent in correctional facilities in Lexington, Kentucky; Marianna, Florida; Pleasanton, California; Danbury, Connecticut; and, lastly, Alderson, West Virginia. While serving that sentence, I had plenty of time to consider my own journey, the role of the church, and my walk with God. I am now truly beginning to understand that our steps are ordered by the Lord—for his glory!

Breaking Down and Rebuilding

I endured both the valleys and mountaintop experiences— and looking back I see God's hand in all that I encountered. Often I felt that God had abandoned me and left me on my own to deal with the hand I'd been dealt. I wondered how I'd ended up locked inside a cold prison cell, and I questioned whether my instinctive survival mechanisms coupled with my faith would equip me for what was ahead. I struggled to get through one day at a time, even as I wondered if I had the strength to do ten years. Where was God, and how did my choices land me here?

My first meltdown was in the county jail known as "Seven Locks," while awaiting sentencing after being found guilty. My experience taught me that there are many stages in the criminal justice process where some form of intervention is needed! After being found guilty, many people consider suicide—struggling with whether they can physically do the time, overcome by feelings of guilt and shame, and aware of the impact their imprisonment will have on their families. Being locked away is the ultimate culture change, and at times it can seem impossible to accept what you see before you.

Here is a time when jail chaplains need to look in on you, to make sure you are not too fragile to go to the next stage. Here is where dorm prayer groups can be so instrumental—thank God I knew him when I went in!

So how did it happen to me—a ten-year federal sentence? I was convicted of a drug conspiracy under federal guidelines because I'd made a phone call to try to get money owed to my son so I could pay his bail. I was not a drug dealer, nor did I have any desire to be any part of the bad choices my son was making. He was young and attracted to the "fast money" and a lifestyle of danger. I was the mother who told her son: "You are not living in my house selling drugs!" Yet that phone call made me a conspirator, as my attempt to collect drug money netted me a 121-month sentence.

Under federal guidelines, I was able to earn fifty-four good days each year, which meant I would have to serve some nine years before being released. My son, "David," was sentenced to forty-five years; another codefendant received thirty years—so I guess you could say I was blessed. I learned why the company you keep is so important, and that's a word I'd like to share with any young girls who want to be known as the "drug dealer's girl." I met many such young women in prison—and they weren't getting any visits from their boyfriends, either. My story should also be a warning to other mothers who know their children are into drug-related activities. We mothers do know—and we must put our foot down! I put my foot down—and I still ended up in prison!

A Time of Questions

When I think back on when I was first sentenced, I remember the kinds of questions that ran through my mind:

> Would my church family understand and support me?
> What would life be like with David serving such a long sentence?

What stigma would I face after release—how would I fit in?

Would the church be judgmental toward me?

What kind of career would I have?

What limitations would I have to live with?

In short, what would my life be like after prison— if I could make it through my sentence?

I was always afraid of who would not be there after my release; in other words, how many of my loved ones would die before I would come home? Too often incarcerated persons are unable to attend the funerals of loved ones because of distance, cost, security level, and a host of other issues. I worried about my loving parents. And, of course, I thought about David—and I ask for your prayers as he continues to serve the forty-five-year sentence he received at age twenty-one. We have had several blessings in the court, and his current release date is 2017.

As an incarcerated single mom whose only son was also serving time, I felt "my whole family" was in prison. I felt like a personal failure as a mother. It's important to remember that mothers are still mothers behind prison walls! We still love our children. We still worry about our children. We still want to know what kind of grades they are making, we want to see how they've grown, want to hear about how their day went.

These basic realities suggest a number of different ways churches can help. Before we tackle the challenges of building relationships with incarcerated women and women returning home, consider these specific ways churches can support woman who are incarcerated:

- Churches can use their buses and vans to provide transportation to local jails and prisons for visitation.
- Because the children and families of incarcerated women often face financial challenges, congregations can provide financial support to the current caregivers of those children. Churches can also put money in the

incarcerated woman's commissary account at the correctional facility so she can purchase toiletries, snacks, paper and pencils, and other basic supplies.

- Church members can volunteer as mentors or tutors for children of incarcerated women. (See chapters 5 and 6 for more on this).

- Congregations can collect school supplies, Christmas presents, winter clothing, and other items for distribution to children of incarcerated mothers.

- Congregations can and should create space for members who are caregivers for children of the incarcerated (especially grandmothers raising grandchildren) to give their testimonies and feel the congregation's support, without stigmatizing the mothers of the children for whom they care.

These are just a few of the many things congregations can do—they just need the vision and the will! If members of a congregation feel uncomfortable initiating these efforts on their own (though I couldn't imagine why they would), then churches can collaborate with a reentry program or other service organization that is already involved in such work. Existing reentry programs constantly seek committed volunteer assistance.

Worry and Faith

Incarcerated mothers worry constantly about their children. We worry about who is raising our kids, regardless of whether our children are in foster care or in the care of other relatives. We wonder if the caretakers are loving our children as we would. We wonder if our kids are being reminded every day of how much we love them, or whether our names are being dragged through the mud. In my own situation, I wondered whether my son would even survive. Women in prison may fight to mess up someone's face or to break the monotony of another day, but the reality is that men sometimes fight to kill.

For me, coping with these worries has a lot to do with faith. I had to believe in the sovereignty of God! If God is Lord of the universe, and if God cares about every detail of my life (and yours), then even this fate will work out for the good. Even if the devil had a plan for my life, God has the final say, just as he did with Job. I had to believe God's plan for me was for "welfare not harm, to give you a future with hope" (Jeremiah 29:11). Other favorite Scriptures got me through, helping me remember "this sickness is not unto death" (John 11:4). I knew God had me!

I learned so much in my quiet place. God did speak and encourage me through even that ordeal. I knew that my son was in God's hands—even when he was rushed to the hospital after some "unexplained" event! I learned to trust God with every fiber of my being. Even when I got pneumonia and almost died—when I was brought into the hospital shackled at the waist, hands, and feet, and watched the attending nurse carefully move her purse from the room I was in—I learned to trust.

Understanding Women's Criminality

Congregations can help by resisting the temptation to stigmatize incarcerated mothers. Instead, churches can help these women see their worth as people created in the image of God, and work to bring them into right relationship with God and family. I faced this challenge on my own—but your congregation can help lovingly alter perceptions by breaking the silence on women's incarceration and show your love by ministering to these women as persons needing redemption and healing.

To really understand a woman's criminal behavior, we must look at her life before incarceration, including any prior history of abuse, relationship problems, and drug use. The reality is that most of the women in prison are there for nonviolent crimes, and even the serious crimes are most often against someone with whom they were intimate. The "war on drugs" contributed to the increase in women's incarceration—yet women's substance use and abuse is often an attempt to medicate pain from trauma they've experienced. At a "What Works in Reentry" roundtable hosted by the Urban Institute in April 2010, Suffolk County (MA) Sherriff Andrea Cabral noted that 70 percent of incarcerated women have experienced some form of past trauma, such as child abuse, sexual assault, or domestic violence. As was the case with my own sentence, women are often sentenced as "accomplices" in criminal activity initiated by men. Reflecting on his own ministry with young women who had been prostitutes in Korea, missions specialist Harvie Conn spoke about how Jesus ministered to "sinners who were sinned against." This same description applies to many women in U.S. prisons today.

When we really try to understand the context of a woman's imprisonment, we find that bad relationships from childhood forward often contribute mightily to the decisions that led to incarceration. It logically follows that women need support for developing new relationships and new ways of forming relationships—while incarcerated, in preparation for returning from incarceration, and while making the transition from incarceration to home and society. A congregation that understands this reality can provide important social supports necessary to move from the simple fact of reentry to the ultimate goal of reintegration into society. If a prison ministry or prisoner reentry ministry just preaches and conducts Bible study, women may get information and inspiration, but they won't necessarily get the transformation needed to build new relationships. Congregations can help teach good relationship building—and that starts with the congregation deciding to build relationships with these women themselves.

A woman returning from incarceration often finds that society continues to reimpose her sentence—when she is looking for a job, if she applies for food stamps, when she seeks to rent an apartment. Her actual time in prison is over, but she continues to face sanctions and negative stigma, when what she needs are opportunities for restoration and reconciliation. By building relationships, congregations can let women know that, though society stigmatizes and judges them, God loves them—and so do the people of God. In doing so, congregations can be agents of justice and healing, helping to restore relationships and find solutions.

Think of how much can be resolved in the church! Remember that the church was once the focal point of the community—especially the African American community. We went to the church as a social service agency before the term came into existence and defined our economic status! Where traditional services for women fail, congregations can provide the relational resources necessary to be reconciled to home and community, a reconciliation that involves both the love and reception of those affected by the offense, and the need for accountability on the part of women convicted of criminal behavior.

Local churches must teach, through example, how to trust God, how to understand God's Word, how to pray, how to let songs minister to our pain, how to forgive others and ourselves, and how to be grateful for the life God has given us! Teams working in prison ministry must show women on the inside how to create support systems among themselves and how to begin to trust other people. Learning to trust again in prison is difficult, but I know it's possible, because I had friends in prison! God puts love in your heart, and you can't help but love others. How do you serve if you cannot love? Even as I served my ten-year sentence, I was grateful—

grateful to see a new day, grateful that God was in my life, grateful that he loved me and that his mercies were new every day. Just plain ol' grateful!

Nurturing Women's Faith

So what does it take for churches to nurture the "woman kind of faith" among women who are incarcerated or in the process of reentry? It involves understanding that women have different needs in reentry, and being women! It includes awareness of the profile and patterns of women's experiences and history, the pathways that often lead women into criminal behavior, and the specific issues that shape female offenders' lives—including gender, environment, relationships, services and supervision, socioeconomic status, and community.

Based on my experience working with churches as part of the National Women's Prison Project, I'd offer the following suggestion to congregations and individuals wanting to support women during incarceration and reentry:

1. Get to know the women who are incarcerated or returning from the criminal justice system. Demonstrate that you really care about their reentry into the community. Let them know you are there not to judge them but to support them.
2. Understand the role of trauma in the lives of so many of the women who find themselves in prison. This will help you to become more forgiving and empathetic. (Chapter 11 addresses this issue.)
3. Recognize your own need for healing even as you minister to others. Reaching out to others who are hurting requires knowing ourselves, both our own brokenness and the places we have experienced healing.

4. Make sure you are willing to help all God's children—not just those who seem like you or those with whom you are comfortable.

5. Minister to women understanding that each of them is part of a family unit, not an isolated being. Minister in the context of family and be prepared to assist the family unit.

6. Know the resources available to assist women in your community—including childcare facilities, transportation, health services, substance abuse aftercare, job training, and family reunification services (to name a few).

7. Identify local places that are willing to hire persons with a criminal background. Help the women prepare for job interviews and become comfortable discussing their backgrounds.

8. Provide transportation! Offer to pick up returning citizens and bring them to church with you, or provide rides (and company) to organizations providing services.

9. Become an advocate. Learn when and how to advocate for the returning-citizen community, and help change archaic laws that continue to persecute and reconvict.

10. Pray with (and for) them! Many women begin or renew their faith journeys while on the inside and want to continue on the outside. Help them know that the faith they have found is real.

If your church has not been trained in working with returning citizens, there are many effective models out there—including those used by Prison Fellowship, Kairos, Healing Communities, Christian Association for Prisoner Aftercare, and others. These organizations can be contacted for advice and support. Your congregation can connect to models that are working, create programming that fits the needs of your congregation, and allow the impacted persons you serve to share their input in growing your ministry!

It is not difficult for the church to minister to returning citizens. We just have to care and then do something. And we must use both kindness and common sense—which means women should minister to women, while men work with men.

The congregation has a voice and a role in shaping what happens when women come home from prison. We need to speak out on behalf of women returning from prison, even as we assist these women in finding their own voices as well. And we need to recognize that the women coming home are our mothers, daughters, and granddaughters; our sisters, aunties, and cousins.

Chapter 8

An Ounce of Prevention

CHARLES E. LEWIS JR.

The focus of much of this book is reentry—helping persons who have been incarcerated successfully reintegrate into society and avoid returning to jail or prison. However, a word is needed about *preentry*—the challenge of helping young people avoid getting ensnared by the criminal justice system in the first place. While reentry strategies and efforts are critical to reducing recidivism and stemming the number of people who return to prison after being released, the best way to reduce prison and jail populations is to prevent young people from engaging in the system at all. If we don't do a better job of this, we will surely be doing reentry programs for a long time. Until we are successful in meeting the psychological, emotional, and behavioral needs of children and adolescents, too many will continue to make the poor choices that get them in trouble.

"Train a child in the way he should go: and when he is old, he will not depart from it" (Proverbs 22:6, KJV). This familiar passage of Scripture is repeated often in African American churches. For many it means children should be involved in Sunday school and other constructive activities that will teach them the moral lessons needed to keep them on the straight and narrow road to success. For others it is an admonition to parents to be diligent in disciplining their children and is often partnered with the age-old warning of "spare the rod and spoil the child."

Unfortunately, too many African American children receive moral training in neither the church nor the home. Absent a stable and loving household, youngsters often learn their values and coping styles from peers, the streets, television, movies, and other influences besides that of a caring adult. We cannot expect schools to provide moral training. And we dare not look to the juvenile justice system to help train our kids, for it has become a system that seeks only to punish and deter, not to rehabilitate.

Understanding the Juvenile Justice System

The first juvenile court, created in Chicago, Illinois, in 1899, was based on a belief that adolescents were not fully accountable and had a diminished understanding of the law. The juvenile justice system that emerged in the early twentieth century was designed to rescue wayward youth and focused on treatment and "the best interests of the child."[1] Youth who found their way into this system were thought to be lacking social and emotional development and were given a remedy of intense school work and counseling.[2]

As arrest rates for juvenile offenders began to climb in the late 1980s and early 1990s, crime watchers—notably Princeton University Professor John Diulio—began warning about a wave of "super predator" teens who would wreak havoc on society.[3] Arrest rates peaked in 1996 at 9,443 per 100,000 youth—up 27 percent from 1980. African American youth were arrested at the rate of 16,647 per 100,000—more than double the arrest rate for white youth. Juvenile arrest rates began to decline in 1997 and are now below 1980 levels.[4]

The peak in juvenile arrests came when the nation was still wrestling with the aftermath of the sensational case of five black teenagers who received stiff prison sentences after being convicted of raping a white jogger in Central Park in 1989. Described as a "wolf pack," they became the poster boys for the very predators criminologists were warning about.[5] Americans were losing their collective appetites for investing in "criminals"—and it did not matter if they were young. The five teenagers were later exonerated when the actual rapist confessed, but their lives were irrevocably damaged by a justice system seeking to make examples of them.[6]

Between 1992 and 2000, forty-five states passed legislation that allowed or made it easier for juveniles to be tried in adult courts. An official estimate in 2000 reported that slightly more than four thousand youth are locked up in adult facilities on any given day—and half of them are in maximum security facilities.[7] Hundreds more rotate in and out of adult jails annually. As many as 200,000 adolescents are prosecuted in the adult criminal justice system over the course of a year.[8] Although a minority of the population, African American and Latino youth represent up to seven of ten youth tried in adult systems.[9]

Such "get tough" policies take a toll on young people. Compared to those in secured juvenile facilities, youth sentenced to adult prisons are more likely to be victimized by both inmates and staff and less likely to receive adequate access to training programs.[10] A felony conviction in adult court will haunt the youthful offender for the rest of his or her life, limiting both education and employment opportunities.

At the same time, the juvenile justice system, once designed to provide structure and discipline to the lives of wayward youth, has now become the gateway to the harsh realities of jails and prisons. Emulating adult criminal justice systems, efforts to provide instruction and correction within the juvenile system have largely been abandoned in favor of a focus on punishment and incapacitation. The juvenile justice system has become the "minor leagues" for young people who seem destined for the big leagues of the adult criminal justice system.

Who Gets Caught in the Criminal Justice System?

For those of us who are concerned about the damage being done to so many African Americans by the criminal justice system, the challenge is to find the means to halt the inexorable march of so many African American youth into the clutches of the police, the courts, and our jails and prisons. If we do not find a way to reduce the numbers going in, we can be certain we will be busy with reentry work until the Second Coming.

So what do we know about the young African Americans who get caught up in the criminal justice system? Let us assume that African American youth are not innately pathological—to assume otherwise would be to condemn black youth to substandard lives from birth. We know that youth who find their way into our justice system are more likely to be poor and to live in neighborhoods that are economically challenged. They are more likely to be products of a single-parent household. They are more likely to be a child of someone engaged in the criminal justice system.

These youth are also more likely to have a diagnosable psychological, emotional, or behavioral problem. Though such problems sometimes have a biological cause, in other cases they are the result of environmental factors or neglect.[11] There is a growing body of evidence that links a child's exposure to violence to a multiplicity of adverse outcomes including antisocial behaviors, post-traumatic stress disorder (PTSD), and substance use.[12] Children's exposure to violence is also associated with future criminal behavior.[13] Recent research on the brain has produced evidence that stress induced by childhood poverty leads to impaired memory functioning of the brain in early adulthood.[14]

As a licensed clinical therapist as well as a parent who has faced the challenge of raising teenagers myself, I know the difficulties of helping youth navigate the treacherous passage from childhood to adulthood. From early adolescence (which begins somewhere around eleven years old), youth are confronted with enormous challenges on a daily basis. They are discovering their own identities and learning to fit into a complex social network. They are learning to handle developing bodies and manage sexual urges. They face peer pressure to experiment with tobacco, alcohol, and other mood-altering substances. They are renegotiating relationships with parents and other adults in their lives. All of this is occurring as they try to deal with school and wonder what kind of future might be awaiting them.[15] Crossing the burning sands of adolescence is a tumultuous experience for all young people. Given the dire circumstances faced by many African American youth, it is understandable that so many fail to reach adulthood without escaping the clutches of the criminal justice system.

Mental health problems are another factor in determining which young people end up in our criminal justice system. A report by the U.S. surgeon general estimates that about one in five children in the United States has a mental health disorder.[16] Without proper intervention, these youngsters are in danger of doing poorly in school, becoming truant, dropping out, and getting caught up in the criminal justice system. Estimates of the number of youth in the juvenile justice system who have a diagnosable mental health disorder reach as high as 70 percent or more.[17]

Once in the juvenile justice system, youth with mental health problems are not likely to receive adequate or appropriate treatment.[18] Budget shortfalls have caused many states to cut back on available mental health services.[19] Yet many parents often view it as their last resort option to get help for their children. A 2003 Government Accountability Office (GAO) report estimated that more than 12,700 parents placed their children with child welfare agencies or juvenile justice systems to obtain mental health services.[20]

By the time children are placed in the care of state and local agencies their lives are usually spiraling out of control. More effort and resources are needed for prevention and early intervention. The Institute of Medicine has highlighted several decades of research supporting the efficacy of preventing mental illness, estimating that as much $247 billion in annual costs could be saved through prevention and early intervention.[21] The failure to provide sufficiently for the psychological, emotional, and behavioral needs of children and adolescents has resulted in thousands of children as young as seven and eight years old being held in secured juvenile facilities for lack of community mental health services.[22]

Supporting Healthy Families

So how do we get in front of this problem? How do we ensure that the psychological, emotional, and behavioral needs of younger children are met so that problems will not escalate as they progress into adolescence? In a perfect world, all children would be born into stable, two-parent households with loving and knowledgeable parents who possess the economic and moral resources needed to nurture their children into citizens of good character. All children would grow up in communities free of crime with well-resourced schools and a myriad of constructive social activities at their disposal. Every child would grow up with a respect for the law and would be surrounded by police officers whose primary concern was providing safety for the citizens of the community and keeping young people out of trouble.

Needless to say, we live in a less than perfect world. Far too many children in the United States are born into single-parent households, and these kids are much more likely to grow up in poverty.[23] Four of every ten children in the United States are born to single mothers, and more than 70 percent of all African American children are born out of wedlock.[24] The amount of poverty is not a reflection on unmarried mothers, but the reality of maintaining a household on a single paycheck. According to U.S. Census data among all races, only 8.6 percent of married couples with children under eighteen years old live below the poverty line, compared to 38.9 percent of children living with a single mother. In white married families, 8.1 percent of children are living below the poverty line, while 34.8 percent of families with a single mom heading the household are living below the poverty line. For black married families, 10.1 percent live below the poverty line, as do 19.8 percent of Hispanic families. But children in nonwhite single-mother headed households are much worse off—with 47.4 percent of black families and 46.3 percent of Hispanic families below the poverty line.[25]

Factor in the added demands of parenting placed on the single mother—particularly those who are raising sons—and you have a recipe for problems. Policy-makers—especially conservatives—are reluctant to offer single mothers too much assistance because they believe providing generous support would reduce the likelihood of mothers deciding to marry. The Bush administration took this policy idea a step further by investing millions of taxpayer dollars into promoting marriage, particularly among low-income households. The Healthy Marriage and Responsible Fatherhood Act of 2006 provided $150 million over five years to conduct programs and workshops promoting healthy marriage and responsible fatherhood. The African American Healthy Marriage Initiative grew out of this effort and has involved African American churches in the effort to create stable two-parent families. Preliminary evidence suggests it is having some success—and the Obama administration is continuing the effort.[26]

The truth is that the vast majority of single mothers are loving and effective parents, but they struggle with fewer resources. They also have less time to spend with their children because of the need to work and the work requirements for those receiving Temporary Assistance for Needy Families (TANF).[27] Criminal justice sanctions have scarred many African American males and reduced their ability to earn a decent living, making them less desirable partners for marriage and forming stable families.[28] While the rewards of marriage are indisputable for adults and children, unless the impediments creating healthy households are addressed in a meaningful way, these realities are not going to change.

The church needs to understand what astute policy-makers know: Promoting marriage is more than convincing two people to tie the knot and providing premarital counseling. There must be policies in place that support fragile families.[29] One example of effective policy is the Earned Income Tax Credit (EITC), which has done much to support low-income families and has lifted millions of these working families out of poverty.[30] Further expansion of the EITC could help additional struggling couples find the will to stay and work together.

Churches have been actively involved in the African American Healthy Marriage Initiative, as well they should. We must do all we can to promote healthy relationships between parents that result in stable and caring families. But what should we do for the children who will not be in a nurturing family?

Churches Serving Troubled Youth

In 1998 the Substance Abuse and Mental Health Services Administration (SAMHSA) began funding "systems of care" under the Comprehensive Community Mental Health Services Program for Children and Their Families. This funding provided a broad range of services for at-risk children and adolescents and their families.[31] But one critical missing element was the active inclusion of churches in the planning and administration of the service plan.

While churches and pastors are often the refuge of first resort for families with "troubled" children, they are generally not actively engaged with secular mental health systems.[32] Religious people are underrepresented in the mental health field, and most mental health professionals receive little or no religious training in their graduate studies. Credentialed professions and disciplines, such as social work and psychology, insist licensing is needed in mental health services as a means to protect people from harm even if services are well intended.

Given the historical mistrust of white health institutions rooted in misguided interventions such as the Tuskegee experiment, it is not surprisingly that African Americans seeking psychological help would prefer to be serviced by a professional of color. Yet African Americans are underrepresented as psychological service providers, which limits the options for referrals by clergy and lay counselors. African Americans represent 1.9 percent of doctoral-level psychologists, 1.6 percent of psychiatrists, 6.4 percent of social workers, and 3.8 percent of counseling professionals.[33]

Churches must take a proactive stance to break through barriers that prevent them from participating in systems of care. They must actively seek opportunities to engage service providers. That means knowing who is providing services in your community, taking an assessment of those services, and determining if the providers are meeting the needs of the community. That sounds like a good plan, but are churches equipped to do this?

Larger congregations may find the needed expertise among their members. Churches in the same neighborhood can work together. If the expertise is not available in your congregation, churches can reach out to schools of social work, nonprofit advocacy groups, or government offices to seek help. Churches can also assist children and families in getting the help they need by providing information, offering access to computers, hosting health fairs, and collaborating with providers.[34]

While churches can have an impact by connecting community residents to available services, they have the potential to have even a greater impact by stepping up their advocacy efforts to influence policies that ensure needed services are provided. It will take the collective voices of African American churches to get the attention of policymakers. Elected officials care about one commodity above all others—votes. When a critical mass of people gets behind an issue, politicians pay attention.

Advocating on behalf of young people and families in need of psychological, emotional and behavioral services does not require churches to become mired in partisan politics. Since most churches are incorporated as nonprofit organizations, the leadership is right to be concerned about jeopardizing the church's tax-exempt status. But there are many activities churches can engage in without endorsing a particular candidate or political party. In chapter 16, "Why Policy Matters," we will say more about this and will provide specific examples of policies that can make a difference.

The bottom line is that disproportionate involvement in the criminal justice system is wreaking havoc on African Americans, our families, and communities. An overwhelming number of African American boys and girls are getting caught in the juvenile justice system at an early age. Too often this occurs because their psychological, emotional, and behavioral needs are not appropriately met. Getting our children the help they need early will go a long way in preventing mental illness and behavioral problems and keep them out of jail and prison.

African American churches cannot abide the status quo. We cannot afford to give less than our fullest effort to reduce the harmful effects of mass incarceration. Ministry to the incarcerated and their families must include not only reentry strategies, but prevention initiatives as well. We need to keep working to rescue people who have fallen in the river, but we must also move upstream and figure out how to keep them from falling into the river in the first place.

▪ NOTES ▪

1. Richard Lawrence and Craig Hemmens, *Juvenile Justice: A Text/Reader* (Thousand Oaks, CA: Sage, 2008), 20; M. Joan McDermott and John H. Laub, "Adolescence and Juvenile Justice Policy," *Criminal Justice Policy Review* 1, no. 4 (1986): 439–40.

2. Steven Gluck, "Wayward Youth, Super Predator." *Corrections Today* 59, no. 3 (1997).

3. John J. DiIulio Jr., "Young and Deadly: The Problem of Juvenile Crime." *National Review*, April 3, 2000, http://web.ebscohost.com.cassell.founders.howard.edu (accessed February 21, 2010).

4. National Center for Juvenile Justice, "Juvenile Arrest Rates by Offense Sex and Race" (Washington, DC: Office of Juvenile Justice Delinquency and Prevention, 2009), http://ojjdp.ncjrs.org/ojstatbb/crime/excel/JAR_2008.xls (accessed February 13, 2010).

5. Michel Marriott, "Harlem Residents Fear Backlash from Park Rape," *New York Times*, April 24, 1989, B3.

6. Simone Weichselbaum, "Still Haunted by 'Wolf Pack' Label," *New York Daily News*, April 12, 2009, 12.

7. James J. Stephan and Jennifer C. Karberg, "Census of State and Federal Correctional Facilities, 2000" (Washington, DC: Bureau of Justice Statistics, 2003), 17.

8. Campaign for Youth Justice, "The Consequences Aren't Minor: The Impact of Trying Youth as Adults and Strategies for Change" (Washington, DC: Justice Policy Institute, 2007), 4, http://www.campaignforyouthjustice.org/Downloads/NEWS/National_Report_consequences.pdf (accessed December 29, 2008).

9. James Austin, Kelly Dedel Johnson, and Maria Gregoriou, "Juveniles in Adult Prisons and Jails" (Washington, DC: Bureau of Justice Statistics, 2000), 40, http://www.ncjrs.gov/pdffiles1/bja/182503.pdf (accessed February 21, 2010).

10. Martin Forst, Jeffrey Fagan, and T. Scott Vivona, "Youth in Prisons and Training Schools: Perceptions and Consequences of the Treatment-Custody Dichotomy," *Juvenile and Family Court Journal* 40, no. 1 (1989): abstract.

11. Lynsay Ayer and James J. Hudziak, "Socioeconomic Risks for Psychopathology: The Search for Causal Mechanisms," *Journal of the American Academy of Child and Adolescent Psychiatry* 48, no. 10 (2009): 982–83.

12. Michael Lynch, "Consequences of Children's Exposure to Community Violence," *Clinical Child and Family Psychology Review* 6, no. 4 (2003): 265–67; Dana D. DeHart and Sandra J. Altshuler, "Violence Exposure among Children of Incarcerated Mothers," *Child Adolescent Social Work Journal* 26 (2009): 467–69.

13. Robert Geffner, Dawn Alley Griffin, and James Lewis, III, "Children Exposed to Violence: An Often Neglected Social, Mental Health and Public Health Problem," *Journal of Emotional Abuse* 8, no. 1/2 (2008): 8.

14. Gary W. Evans and Michelle A. Schamberg, "Childhood Poverty, Chronic Stress and Adult Memory," *Proceedings of the National Academy of Sciences* 106 (2009): 3, http://www.pnas.org/content/early/2009/03/27/0811910106.full.pdf+html (accessed February 21, 2010).

15. For an insightful understanding of adolescent brain development, see David Walsh, *Why Do They Act That Way: A Survival Guide to the Adolescent Brain for You and Your Teen* (New York: Free Press, 2004), 2.

16. U.S. Department of Health and Human Services, "A Report of the Surgeon General—Chapter 3: Children's Mental Health" (Washington, DC: Author, 1999), 123–24, http://www.surgeongeneral.gov/library/mentalhealth/pdfs/c3.pdf (accessed February 23, 2010).

17. Richard F. Dalton, Lisa J. Evans, Keith R. Cruise, Ronald A. Feinstein, and Rhonda F. Kendrick, "Race Differences in Mental Health Service Access in a Secure Male Juvenile Justice Facility," *Journal of Offender Rehabilitation* 48 (2009): 194–95.

18. Steven J. Osterlind, James R. Koller, and Edwin F. Morris, "Incidence and Practical Issues of Mental Health for School-Aged Youth in Juvenile Detention," *Journal of Correctional Health Care* 13, no. 4 (2007): 276–77.

19. National Association of State Mental Health Program Directors, "SMHA Budget Shortfalls: FY 2009, 2010 & 2011" (Washington, DC: Author, 2008), http://www.nri-inc.org/reports_pubs/2009/Budget Shortfalls.pdf (accessed February 23, 2010).

20. Government Accountability Office (GAO), "Child Welfare Agencies and Juvenile Justice Systems," report no. GAO-03-397 (Washington, DC: Author, 2003), 14, http://www.gao.gov/new.items/d03397.pdf (accessed February 23, 2010).

21. Institute of Medicine, "Preventing Mental, Emotional, and Behavioral Disorders among Young People: Progress and Possibilities—Executive Summary (Washington, DC: National Academy of Sciences, 2009), 1–2, http://www.nap.edu/catalog/12480.html (accessed February 28, 2010).

22. U.S. House of Representatives Committee on Government Reform, "Incarceration of Youth Who Are Waiting for Mental Health Services in the United States" (Washington, DC: Author, 2004), 4–5, http://www.hsgac.senate.gov/public/index.cfm (accessed February 23, 2010).

23. Paul R. Amato and Rebecca A. Maynard, "Decreasing Nonmarital Births and Strengthening Marriage to Reduce Poverty," *The Future of Children* 17, no. 2 (2007): 118–19; Nicholas H. Wolfinger, Lori Kowaleski-

Jones, and Ken R. Smith, "Family Structure Transitions and Child Achievement," *Sociological Spectrum* 28 (2008): 698.

24. National Center for Health Statistics, "Health, United States, 2008," (Hyattsville, MD: Author, 2009), 172, http://www.cdc.gov/nchs/hus.htm (accessed January 31, 2010).

25. U.S. Census Bureau, "Current Population Survey POV03: People in Families with Related Children Under 18 by Family Structure, Age, Sex, Iterated by Income-to-Poverty Ratio and Race," http://www.census.gov/hhes/www/cpstables/032009/pov/new03_100.htm (accessed February 23, 2010).

26. Mary Myrick, Theodora Ooms, and Patrick Patterson, "Healthy Marriage and Relationship Programs: A Promising Strategy for Strengthening Families" (Washington, DC: National Healthy Marriage Resource Center, 2009), http://www.acf.hhs.gov/healthymarriage (accessed January 31, 2010).

27. In 1996 President Bill Clinton signed the Personal Responsibility and Work Opportunity Reconciliation Act (Public Law 104-193) that reformed traditional welfare entitlements provided by Aid to Families with Dependent Children (AFDC). The new law created the Temporary Assistance for Needy Families (TANF) program that included work requirements for mothers receiving assistance and set time limits for receiving benefits.

28. Charles E. Lewis Jr., "Incarceration and Family Formation," in *Social Work with African American Males: Health, Mental Health, and Social Policy*, ed. Waldo E. Johnson Jr. (New York: Oxford University Press, 2010).

29. "Fragile families" is a term coined by Columbia University professor Ronald B. Mincy to describe low-income couples during the early stages of family formation.

30. The Earned Income Tax Credit is a refundable tax credit for low-income working families with children designed to boost incomes and offset payroll taxes. Enacted in 1975, it provided a maximum credit of $3,043 for families with one child and a maximum credit of $5,038 for families with two children in 2009. The maximum credit is $5,667 for families with three or more children. As a refundable credit, if the families' tax burden is less than the credit, the difference is refunded to the taxpayers. Although the EITC has lifted millions out of poverty, between 15 percent and 25 percent of eligible taxpayers fail to apply for the credit, leaving 3.5 to 7 million eligible families without the benefit. For a fuller description of the EITC, visit the IRS website at http://www.irs.gov.

31. For more information on systems of care, visit http://systemsofcare.samhsa.gov/.

32. Andrew J. Weaver, "Mental Health Professionals Working with Religious Leaders," in *Handbook of Religion and Mental Health*, ed. Harold G. Keonig (London: Academic Press, 1998), 350–51; Christopher G. Ellison, Margaret L. Vaaler, Kevin J. Flannelly, and Andrew J. Weaver, "The

Clergy as a Source of Mental Health Assistance: What Americans Believe," *Review of Religious Research* 48, no. 2 (2006): 190–91.

33. Darryl L. Townes, Shannon Chavez-Korrell, and Nancy J. Cunningham, "Reexamining the Relationships between Racial Identity, Cultural Mistrust, Help-Seeking Attitudes, and Preference for a Black Counselor," *Journal of Counseling Psychology* 56, no. 2 (2009): 330.

34. Charles E. Lewis Jr., and Harold Dean Trulear, "Rethinking the Role of African American Churches as Social Service Providers," *Black Theology* 6, no. 3 (2008): 355–56.

Chapter 9

Substance Abuse and Incarceration

SYLVIA MOSELEY ROBINSON

My heart ached as I listened to the petite, baby-faced, twenty-one-year-old recount the story of her latest arrest for prostitution. She spoke of how she had prayed for help—and how God rescued her in the person of a Dayton police officer posing as a john. As I listened to her story and surveyed the upturned faces of the other women in this Bible study at Montgomery County Jail, the Holy Spirit brought a Scripture to my memory that states, "There is a path before each person that seems right, but it ends in death" (Proverbs 14:12, NLT). None of these women started out in first grade aspiring to become a drug addict who would spend her youth selling her body on the streets of Dayton, Ohio. How did their lives spiral downward to bring them to this point? How many found themselves in this condition because of circumstances of birth? How many made poor choices until they lost hope of ever seeing anything different for themselves?

Whether people find themselves addicted and incarcerated because of bad choices, sexual abuse, unrelenting poverty, poor parenting skills, or (as the church is so fond of saying) "generational curses," incarceration and substance abuse have become strongholds in the lives of millions. Many have re-signed themselves to patterns of destructive behavior they feel unable to escape. I understand this personally, because I was once captive to a lifestyle that told me, "It's your thing; do what you want to do with it." Such thinking shaped and molded me during a formative time in Brooklyn, New York, and this led me to make many foolish choices in the years that followed.

After years of futile attempts to live successfully with drugs, I cried out to God and surrendered my life to him. I can say that I've lived out the old hymn's words, "I once was lost but now am found." But there are millions in our prisons who still need to experience God's amazing grace. In the face of rampant substance abuse and mass incarceration, the church of Jesus Christ has a unique opportunity to march into prisons across this country and share God's saving love with those who do not know Jesus.

God is still performing miracles; I see evidence of this in the hundreds of thousands who have been set free from the seemingly hopeless state of substance abuse and incarcera-tion. And God is using the transformed lives of those who have been set free—sending them into prisons with a message of hope that meets people at their point of need. We've expe-rienced this in our own ministry at Dayton's Omega Baptist Church, under the leadership of Rev. Dr. Daryl Ward and Rev. Vanessa Oliver Ward, where God has paved the way for our outreach work at the local prison. Initially, like other church prison ministries, we taught Bible studies, preached, and led broken souls to make confessions of faith in Christ. But it quickly became apparent that, in addition to whatever spiritual, social, moral, or educational struggles the inmates had, substance abuse was often a core problem.

Drug Abuse and Prisons

An ever-increasing number of the people in prisons and jails across this country are struggling with drug-related problems. Many of the battered and broken lives we encounter in the Montgomery County Jail are first-, second-, and third-generation substance abusers who, driven by their obsession to use drugs, get involved in myriad other offenses, including selling drugs, selling their bodies, destroying property, and engaging in acts of child abuse or domestic violence. Those of us working inside the jails, prisons, prerelease centers, and other front lines of this struggle recognize it as a spiritual war. In 2 Corinthians 10:3-5 (NLT), Paul writes, "We are human, but we don't wage war with human plans and methods. We use God's mighty weapons, not mere worldly weapons to knock down the devil's strongholds. With these weapons we break down every proud argument that keeps people from knowing God."

Christians engaged in ministry to incarcerated substance abusers realize the forces we battle are more than mere flesh and blood. Drug addiction is a malady that has entrapped individuals physically, mentally, and spiritually. In his article "Addiction Is a Brain Disease," Alan I. Lasher states:

> A core concept that has been evolving with scientific advances over the past decade is that drug addiction is a brain disease that develops over time because of the initially voluntary behavior of using drugs. The consequence is virtually uncontrollable compulsive drug craving, seeking, and use that interferes with, if not destroys, an individual's functioning in the family and in society. This medical condition demands formal treatment. We now know in detail the brain mechanisms through which drugs acutely modify mood, memory, perception, and emotional states. Using drugs repeatedly over time changes brain structure and function in fundamental and long-lasting ways that can persist long after the individual stops using them.[1]

Thousands caught in the grip of addiction admit the need for a higher power and find themselves in 12-step programs such as Alcoholics Anonymous and Narcotics Anonymous.

While some churches have provided meeting spaces for these programs, other congregations have shunned these fellowships without fully understanding the degree to which 12-step programs draw on the power of God working in the lives of individuals. Six of the twelve steps speak either directly or indirectly of God while only two speak of addiction, addicts, alcohol, or drugs.[2]

Clearly, those intimately acquainted with drug addiction recognize it is a spiritual battle against the powerful forces of evil, yet the U.S. criminal justice system continues to respond to it with carnal weapons. The human cost of this approach has been an overwhelming number of broken lives.

Drug Sentencing and Incarceration

The war on drugs has fueled the exploding prison population in urban America. Until the 1970s, virtually every state employed indeterminate sentencing in its criminal justice system. This allowed judges some latitude in determining sentencing and allowed for inmates to be considered for parole based on their behavior in prison. This sentencing structure gave incarcerated persons an incentive to take advantage of educational, vocational, and spiritual programming offered in the prison, which could lead to early release.[3]

In the 1970s, in the face of increasing crime rates, indeterminate sentencing faced attacks from both liberal and conservatives. The Right argued that the crime rate could be cut in half simply by eliminating early release policies that benefited violent criminals who were "going free in droves."[4] The Left attacked the great variations in sentencing that showed evidence of biases based on race, class, and gender. And both sides raised questions about the effectiveness of rehabilitation programs for offenders in the face of "research" among adult and juvenile offenders that proved these efforts failed to change the behavior of the criminally inclined. In the minds of many, this justified harsher and longer sentences.[5]

In 1973, the state legislature of New York set the tone for the nation by passing the Rockefeller Drug Laws, which included mandatory prison terms for illegal drug offenses. These laws meant longer prison terms and very limited plea bargaining for drug offenses.[6] Other states soon followed suit. The 1980 election of Ronald Reagan began the federal war on drugs and heightened the "get tough on crime" rhetoric. The 1984 Sentencing Reform Act established federal sentencing guidelines that mandated a heavy presumption of imprisonment without regard for any extenuating circumstances.

The Anti–Drug Abuse Act of 1988 stated that its national policy was to "create a drug-free America by 1995." Among its many provisions were mandatory sentences for drug offenses and a special provision to handle the crack epidemic that was sweeping across the country. Based on the assumption that crack was fifty times more addictive than powder cocaine, Congress devised a sentencing policy for crack and powder cocaine that was a 100:1 quantity ratio. A conviction for 500 grams of powder cocaine would result in a five-year mandatory sentence, while just five grams of crack cocaine would trigger the same mandatory sentence.[7]

The human costs of this war on crime and drugs have been devastating for the African American community. In *Malign Neglect: Race, Crime and Punishment in America*, Michael Tonry argues that although criminal behavior by blacks has not been getting worse since the mid-1970s, America's war on drugs has resulted in a steady and disproportionate increase in the numbers and percentages of black inmates. Tonry argues that this could have been foreseen when the war on drugs was declared.[8]

Drug offenders and nonviolent criminals have found themselves on the receiving end of harsher and longer sentences. The number of women in prison has increased dramatically in recent years, and the majority of this increase has consisted of African American women arrested for nonviolent crimes. The U.S. Sentencing Commission and the Department of Justice have concluded that only 5.5 percent of all federal

crack cocaine defendants and 11 percent of federal drug defendants are high-level drug dealers. According to their best
assessment, mandatory minimum sentencing has yielded the
following results:

- *Prison Overcrowding*: While the number of drug us-
  ers imprisoned increased 1,100 percent between 1980
  and 2005, six in 10 people in state prisons on drug
  offenses have no violent history or high-level drug selling activity. And marijuana possession accounted for
  42.6 percent of all drug arrests in 2005, according to
  The Sentencing Project, a liberal prison reform group,
  which used FBI statistics.
- *Racial Injustice*: In 1986, prior to enacting the federal mandatory drug laws, African American drug
  convictions were 11 percent higher than drug convictions of whites; four years later the average federal
  drug sentence for African Americans was 49 percent
  higher.
- *Women*: The incarceration of women has increased
  by 421 percent, and the reality is that 70 percent of
  the female population are low-level nonviolent drug
  offenders.[9]

Clearly, drug use and addiction play a part in much criminal
behavior. Statistics from a U.S. Bureau of Justice Statistics
Special Report revealed that 56 percent of male inmates in
state prisons and 50 percent of federal male inmates reported
drug use within the month prior to their offense. The percentage of women inmates reporting drug use a month prior to
the offense was 45 percent. Finally, "in 2004 an estimated
333,000 prisoners were held for drug violations, 21 percent
of state inmates, and 55 percent of federal inmates."[10]

The mass incarceration of low-level substance abusers
and street dealers has filled our nation's prisons and jails with
nonviolent offenders, further destabilized struggling urban

areas, and increased the burden of incarceration on taxpayers. Yet the imprisonment of more than 2 million people has had little impact on the flourishing illegal drug trade in the United States or around the world.

The average cost to incarcerate one person in federal prison is $21,601 per year. According to a 2002 estimate from the Office of National Drug Control Policy, the annual economic cost of drug abuse was estimated at approximately $181 billion, with an average annual increase of 5.3 percent. This estimate factors in the cost of health and crime consequences, both of which include the loss of productivity due to disability, death, and withdrawal from the legal workforce. The large annual increases in costs are the result of increasing rates of law enforcement, adjudication, and incarceration. It is estimated that $36.4 billion per year of the total costs attributed to drug abuse were primarily utilized on criminal justice system and crime victim costs. The largest portion of these costs ($14.2 billion) found its way into the operating budgets of state and federal corrections, while $9.8 billion went to state and local police operating budgets.[11] At tremendous human and material capital costs, the war on drugs has been a resounding failure.

The thirty-year war on drugs has resulted in the unnatural and unjust dependence on prisons to address what is essentially a social, medical, and spiritual crisis of unprecedented proportions. Such policies have disproportionately affected urban communities and people of color. Melvin Delgado in his book *Where Have All the Young Men and Women of Color Gone?*, notes that social scientists have sounded the alarm as to the futility and dire consequences of the government's war on drug policy:

> The war on drugs would only succeed in increasing criminal justice budgets and imprisoning "non-violent" and "victimless moral" offenders. Such an approach, needless to say, would not have a significant impact on substance abuse!

Currie (1998) states that the increasing use of prisons as "America's social agency" of first resort for coping with the deepening problems of society will have disastrous consequences for the country. Curtis (1992) goes on to argue that antidrug policies have shifted the role of the federal government from investing in youth and people to containing and punishing them, with incarceration being one of the consequences. Such an approach takes a tremendous amount of resources from other areas and instead invests them in controlling significantly larger and larger groups of people, particularly those that are poor and of color.[12]

What Can the Church Do?

What can the church do to respond to the mental, physical, and spiritual struggles of the chronic addict? There are no easy answers, and sometimes these situations can feel hopeless. But Jesus does his best work in "hopeless" situations! Lazarus had been in the grave four days; a sick man had been lying near the pool of Bethesda for thirty-eight years; the woman caught in the act of adultery was about to be executed by men who had stones in their hands. But Jesus entered each of these situations, bringing healing and new life.

Today the church of Christ has an opportunity to be light and salt among people facing similarly dismal situations. Many churches are investing their resources in teaching and preaching a message of hope and healing to persons in jails and prisons around the country. Others have invested their resources in developing programs to mentor inmates while in prison.

When it comes to people whose drug problems have led to their imprisonment, experience has shown that church outreach and support are most effective when they are offered while people are incarcerated. A prison or jail sentence offers an opportunity to reassess one's direction, choices, and lifestyle. Living in an environment where your humanity is diminished and you are reduced to a number is humbling, but minds and spirits are more receptive to new ideas and change in this context as opposed to on the streets.

Inmates have overwhelmingly embraced 12-step Bible studies, making use of *The Life Recovery Bible*, which meets them at their point of need. This Bible, which uses the New Living Translation (NLT), guides the reader in synthesizing the 12 steps of recovery with the Word of God. (Since most inmates tested at no more than a sixth-grade reading level,[13] the King James Version is often beyond their comprehension.) *The Life Recovery Bible* includes seven lessons from the Scriptures for each of the 12 steps, as well eighty-four Bible-based devotionals created around the 12 steps. The topical index includes fifty-six recovery themes with reflections and references that assist readers in finding the correct Scriptures. This Bible helps readers see how their own struggles are mirrored by those of the characters in Scripture. For example, one lesson looks at Samson as he struggles with issues of self-centeredness, powerlessness, and denial of a compulsion he could not control until it led to physical deformity and incarceration.[14]

Omega Baptist Church includes in its annual budget the cost of providing copies of *The Life Recovery Bible* as a resource to be utilized in our jail ministry. We've also sent out a call to other area churches asking for their monetary support to help supply this Bible to various jails, prisons, and institutions. Our ministry serves a number of different weekly 12-step Bible studies, including one at STOP (Secure Transitional Offender Program) a forty-two-bed community correctional facility for men who have committed nonviolent substance abuse offenses, another at a Salvation Army adult rehabilitation center, and a third 12-step Bible study open to the community.

Inmates who grudgingly come to Bible study often light up as they identify for the first time with the people of Scripture and their imperfections and challenges. Their spirits are awakened, and they see the relevance of God's Word to their lives and struggles. Jesus is no longer hidden from the chronic addict, as he reaches out to them in compassion rather than making them feel like pariahs. The Bible chronicles humanity's first, chronic, and fatal addiction—its centuries-old addiction to sin in its many manifestations—and declares God's message of compassion, hope, and salvation. Inmates who would never even pick up a Bible or who had the mistaken concept of God as angry and punishing, are now reading, studying, and sometimes even stealing *The Life Recovery Bible*.

Some church people are unwilling to recognize the ways God is using 12 Step programs to do his work. They perceive Narcotics Anonymous and Alcoholics Anonymous as "cults" and don't support addicts' need to attend support group meetings once they have accepted Christ, telling them, "All you need is Jesus." A few share their own testimonies of how they asked Jesus to remove the taste for drugs, alcohol, tobacco, and loose women, and those cravings were suddenly and miraculously gone. But this is not the testimony of a large number of addicted people. In the Bible, Jesus does not heal every person in the exact same way. We need to ask, "Why are Christians often locked into one model of healing, one way of doing things?" The conflict between church acceptance and support group meetings has led to relapse and return to crime for many addicts. When the church denies the recovering addict acceptance, loving empathy, and encouragement in attending support group meetings, when we are unwilling to address the real challenges of addiction, when we refuse to meet people at their point of need, we are failing to be the church.

Over the last ten years, I have seen how the honesty, open-mindedness, and willingness of men and women coming out of jails and prisons to examine their lives in 12-step Bible studies has yielded fruits of freedom from drugs and committed lives for Christ. I have seen addicts find healing and recovery, acknowledge God's call to the ministry, and then become active members of churches where they initiate their own

12-step Bible studies. I know that Christian recovery literature, support groups, and Bible studies are ways the churches are helping to bridge the gap and reach those who may have thought they were beyond the grace of God.

Many churches around the country have recognized the value of community and love found in support groups. They have initiated Bible studies that speak directly to the needs of those struggling with addiction, both inside prisons and on the outside. I believe the church is the best chance to effect transformation in our communities. Just as the church has come to recognize the need to offer support groups for survivors of cancer, divorce, miscarriage, and many other challenges, we must also provide safe places where those coming out of prison and battling with substance abuse can experience God's love and true community.

Many websites provide valuable information and resources for both prison ministry and Christians in recovery. Here are just a few:

http://christians-in-recovery.org/
http://www.clergyrecovery.com/
http://www.saddleback.com/aboutsaddleback/
signatureministries/celebraterecovery/
http://www.sentencingproject.org/template/index.cfm
http://www.episcopalrecovery.org/
http://www.prisonfellowship.org/prison-fellowship-home
http://www.justicefellowship.org/justice-fellowship-home
http://www.nacronline.com/
http://alcoholism.about.com/cs/christ/a/aa990728.htm
http://www.christianrecoveryministries.com/

▪ NOTES ▪

1. Alan I. Leshner, "Addiction Is a Brain Disease," *Issues in Science and Technology* 17, no. 3 (2001): 75.

2. Alcoholics Anonymous, *The Big Book* (New York: Alcoholics Anonymous World Services, Inc., 1939), 59.

3. Marc Mauer, *Race to Incarcerate* (New York: New Press, 1999), 45.

4. Ibid., 47.

5. Gary Lafree, "Social Institutions and the Crime "Bust" of the 1990s," *Journal of Criminal Law and Criminology* 88, no. 4 (1998): 1358–59.

6. Mauer, *Race to Incarcerate*, 58.

7. Michael Coyle, "*Report to Congress: Cocaine and Federal Sentencing Policy*" (Washington, DC: United States Sentencing Commission, 2002). http://www.ussc.gov/r_congress/02crack/execsumm.pdf (accessed April 13, 2010).

8. Michael Tonry, *Malign Neglect: Race, Crime, and Punishment in America* (New York: Oxford University Press, 1995), 4.

9. Drug Policy Alliance Network, "What's Wrong with the War on Drugs? Mandatory Minimum Sentences," http://www.drugpolicy.org/drugwar/mandatorymin/ (accessed October 8, 2009).

10. Christopher J. Mumola and Jennnifer C. Karberg, "Drug Use and Dependence, State and Federal Prisons, 2004" (Washington DC: Bureau of Justice Statistics, 2006), 1. http://bjs.ojp.usdoj.gov/content/pub/pdf/dudsfp04.pdf (accessed April 13, 2010).

11. Office of National Drug Control Policy, "The Economic Costs of Drug Abuse in the United States, 1992–2002" (Washington, DC: Executive Office of the President, 2004), http://www.ncjrs.gov/ondcppubs/publications/pdf/economic_costs.pdf (accessed April 13, 2010).

12. Melvin Delgado, *Where Are All The Young Men and Women of Color?* (New York: Columbia University Press, 2001), 46.

13. Florida Department of Corrections, "Inmates Tested at Around the 6th Grade Level," http://www.dc.state.fl.us/pub/annual/0607/stats/ia_grade_level.html (accessed October 8, 2009)

14. The Life Recovery Bible (Wheaton, IL: Tyndale, 1998), 313.

Chapter 10

Facilitating Connectedness between Families and Incarcerated Individuals

VERONICA CRAWFORD LYNCH

When a mother or father goes to jail or prison, the entire family unit is disrupted. Relationships are severed temporarily or—in some cases—permanently. Churches are a natural refuge for children whose parents are incarcerated and have an incontrovertible responsibility to act as a catalyst for healing families and restoring connections. Part of the rationale for this mission lies in Matthew 25:31-34 where Jesus talks about providing food for the hungry, care for the sick, and visitation to the imprisoned. Throughout Matthew 25, Jesus' use of metaphor suggests the idea that as followers of the Word, we are ambassadors and advocates for his grace toward the wounded. These ideas support the widely held biblical principle "What you do for the least of these, you do for me." While there is much the church can do, the first place to begin facilitating connectedness between children and their parents is with information by establishing faith-based advocacy committees with the primary purpose of learning as much as they can about public policy, mental health, economic, and child welfare issues.

Child welfare professionals are deeply concerned about the ever-growing number of children who have parents in prison. With more than 2.3 million people locked up in our nation's prisons and jails on any given day, it has been estimated that more than 1.7 million U.S. children have a parent in prison or jail.[1] The children and families impacted by incarceration exist as collateral damage in a war that is raging within many communities.[2] As Phillips and Bloom have noted, "By getting tough on crime, the United States has also gotten tough on children."[3]

Given the huge racial disparities in our prison population, it's not surprising that African American children are disproportionately affected by parental imprisonment. In fact, African American children are seven and a half times more likely to have a parent in prison than European American children.[4] Regardless of how we might feel about the moral decisions and social forces that have led to the incarceration of so many African American parents, the merits of maintaining family connections needs to be based on what is in the best interest of the child. Current evidence suggests that a child will benefit psychologically and emotionally from maintaining contact with the incarcerated parent.[5] Research on children of incarcerated parents shows that family visits are vital to maintaining ties, bolstering children's well-being and healthy development, reducing the trauma of separation, and assisting families after a parent's release.

While many parent-child relationships are permanently severed during incarceration, many other mothers and fathers in prison work hard to maintain the connections with their children and plan to join their families upon release. Nevertheless, they face significant impediments that affect their ability to keep the family together, such as substance abuse problems, mental health issues, poor educational opportunities, and sporadic employment histories.[6] At the same time, the lack of cohesive child welfare and criminal justice policies leaves many children and other family members with nowhere to turn as they seek to cope with the shame and social stigma of a parent's incarceration. There is an urgent need to highlight the issues faced by these families and to reinforce family ties through the development of community linkages and family support programs.

WHAT WE KNOW ABOUT FAMILIES AFFECTED BY INCARCERATION

One in five U.S. families has been touched by the criminal justice system.

Fifty-five percent of male prisoners are fathers of children under the age of eighteen.

Approximately 75 percent of incarcerated women are mothers, and two-thirds have children under the age of eighteen.

Prior to prison, many incarcerated parents were caring and in the lives of their children.

Family members may be the best resource for an incarcerated individual during and after release.

About 8 million children are estimated to have experienced the incarceration of a parent.[7]

Collateral Damage:
Children Serving Time on the Outside

Even in situations where parental substance abuse, poverty, and family violence have previously shaped a child's life, a parent's incarceration can turn the child's world upside down. The imprisonment of a parent can be a lethal blow to a family system that is already severely injured and on life support.

When parents are incarcerated, their children are often thrust into the child welfare system, forced to cope with abrupt, uncertain caregiver arrangements and economic insecurity.[8] Even if the parent was not living in the same household as the child, imprisonment can result in the loss of financial assistance, as well as childcare and social support. Children of incarcerated parents often experience emotional injury, anxiety, depression, and PTSD symptoms.[9] When periods of separation are considerably lengthy, children can develop significant academic and behavioral problems, potentially placing them at a greater risk for delinquency and court involvement.[10]

The stigma associated with incarceration also consigns children and other family members to subordinate societal positions, making them more vulnerable to mental health problems and the disintegration of the family unit.[11] Children separated from parents due to incarceration oftentimes suffer many of the same adverse mental health effects seen in children separated from a parent due to divorce, foster care placement, or death. This is due in part to the fact that children have the ability to remember the traumatic event but do not yet have the psychological skills to process the deep pain and anguish of the parent's arrest and incarceration. Consequently, the trauma of parental incarceration often reveals itself in a child's experiencing parental overidentification, survivor guilt, or even forced silence. Children whose parents are involved in the criminal justice system often exist in the shadows like ghosts, remaining relatively invisible not only to the court system but also to many child welfare agencies and foster care systems. Cuts in government funding have reduced the availability and accessibility of both mental health services and family reunification programs.[12] All these factors unite to create problems not just for incarcerated individuals and their families but for society in general, as returning prisoners attempt to reconnect with families that have not had the social and psychological supports to adequately prepare for their return.

Nonetheless, we must work with the child welfare and criminal justice systems to help children maintain connections with an incarcerated parent, since this can help sustain a child as he or she deals emotionally with the reality of the separation.[13] This is one reason programs that enable visits between kids and incarcerated parents are so important. But we must not overlook the important role that other familial and interpersonal relationships play in attempting to maintain relational connections for both male and female offenders.[14] Many reentry initiatives focus on building and maintaining relationships, because the social and emotional support the returning citizen receives from family and friends will be a significant source of healing and redemption. Despite the fact that many offenders share a history of disrupted and dysfunctional interpersonal relationships, attachments between family members are known to be the core around which most other significantly positive relationships are established.

WHEN THE MOTHER IS INCARCERATED

While the incarceration of either parent is a huge issue in the life of a child, the loss of the mother is of particular significance, since she is more often a child's primary caregiver. Due in part to the war on drugs, the number of women incarcerated in U.S. jails and prisons saw a 53 percent increase between 1995 and 2004.[15] Nearly three-quarters of incarcerated women are mothers, and more than two-thirds have children under the age of eighteen. When a mother is incarcerated, her children are more likely to live with their grandparent or other relatives or friends than with their fathers. Additionally, single women are at increased risk for termination of their parental rights as a result of incarceration and lengthy sentences meted out for drug offenses.[16]

While children of either gender may feel the loss of their mother in a profound manner, adolescent girls may be impacted to the greatest degree. For many young girls, a mother's emotional support speaks to foundational issues regarding the girl's own sense of value and worth as a person as well as her ability to cope effectively with life problems. But for many mothers and daughters already estranged by familial troubles, the canyon created by incarceration can seem impossible to cross.

In its ideal form, the mother-daughter relationship is a nurturing and affectionate bond that provides both mother and daughter with a sense of love and care. Yet even when the relationship has been disrupted or dysfunctional, most daughters long to have an emotionally connected and supportive relationship with their mother and primary caregiver. This is principally because the root of most socialization experiences for women lies in the development of the attachment behavioral system between mother and child.[17]

Compelling research has characterized the attachment between mother and child as both complex and persuasive. Hence, this essential parental relationship should be given the utmost clinical integrity by taking a closer, more pragmatic examination of its correlation to other variables associated with successfully maintaining the connectedness between parent and child during parental incarceration.[18]

WHEN THE FATHER IS INCARCERATED

Whereas children whose mothers are incarcerated are more likely to live with a grandparent or other extended family, children whose fathers are incarcerated most often reside with their mothers. Although incarcerated fathers are less likely than mothers to have resided with their minor children prior to incarceration,[19] even those who don't live with their children prior to arrest often express strong feelings of attachment to their children and hope to be reunited with them upon release. Yet the majority of incarcerated fathers reported no form of weekly contact with their children—which is not surprising since most parents are incarcerated more than one hundred miles away from their family of origin. In fact, the majority of incarcerated fathers serve their entire sentence without ever having a personal visit with their child.

Studies by the Bureau of Justice indicate that most fathers who are incarcerated strongly identify with their role as fathers and desire to maintain a relationship with their children. It is noteworthy that, while many of these fathers did not live with their children prior to incarceration, they often contributed in some way to the financial viability of the family prior to incarceration, and actively sought ways to improve their parenting skills while incarcerated by participating in parenting programs directed by corrections officials.

Maintaining Child-Parent Connections during Incarceration

Survey data indicate that contact between children and their incarcerated parents is irregular or nonexistent. More than half the inmates with minor children say their children have never visited them during their incarceration. Difficulty in maintaining contact between child and parent can be due to factors such as unaffordable collect call charges, hostile and restrictive prison visiting policies, remote and hard to visit prison locations, and strained family relationships.

Mothers in prison stay in touch with their children more than fathers in prison, and African American parents maintain connections more than parents of other ethnicities. Maintaining contact through phone calls is helpful (there are advantages and disadvantages). The availability of different methods of communication will make a difference. Distance matters—the farther the prison is from the child's home, the less likely there will be visitation. Non-friendly policies and practices impact the visitation experience for children and other family members.

Some practitioners question whether children should visit an incarcerated parent. The reluctance of a caregiver or case manager to facilitate a child's visit to the incarcerated parent may be due in part to behavioral and emotional problems that are sometimes exhibited after a visit. It is important to note that children's reactions are often related to the history of continuous and or sporadic disruptions that preceded the arrest of the parent.

While there are valid reasons why some caregivers and social service professionals might limit or eliminate contact between an incarcerated parent and his or her child, in most cases children and families benefit from maintaining contact with an incarcerated parent. Decisions about parent-child contact during incarceration need to serve the best interest of the child first and foremost. Each situation should be considered individually, factoring in both the child's desires as well as whether the parent–child relationship would be supported if the parent were not imprisoned.

Churches can help facilitate contact between children and incarcerated parents in a variety of ways. Here are some additional steps churches can take to assist children and families impacted by incarceration:

- Develop or support structured parent-child visiting programs (such as Girl Scouts Behind Bars).
- Galvanize mental health professionals within the church and local community to provide counseling services for youth who need an outlet to talk freely about their experiences.
- Develop prison-based initiatives that help inmates think about the needs of their children and how to parent from a distance.
- Encourage efforts to create child-friendly visiting areas (or special visiting areas for children), that can directly affect the frequency with which children visit their incarcerated parents.

- Emphasize the primacy of the parenting and caregiver role when designing community outreach programs.
- Work with parents and the legal community to ensure that the parental rights of mothers and fathers are not terminated prematurely.

As more pastors and people begin to realize how widespread the impact of mass incarceration policies reach into their congregations and communities, the need to protect children whose parents have been locked up will be apparent. While mentoring programs have been the principal way the church has helped in the past, new out-of-the-box initiatives need to be considered. One idea would be to develop partnerships with either media outlets or libraries to set up high speed videoconferencing so that children can connect with loved ones through the Internet.

Establishing Christ-centered temporary housing for families upon release is another idea with merit. Also, starting summer camp programs that address issues that are specific to the needs of children with incarcerated parents could be useful. Of primary importance is realizing how crucial the sacred character of the church is to the psychological and emotional growth of these children. Churches can cultivate the minds of youth to heal their spiritual brokenness and support the integrity of the family separated by incarceration.

▪ NOTES ▪

1. Lauren E. Glaze and Laura M. Maruschak, "Parents in Prison and Their Minor Children" (Washington, DC: Bureau of Justice Statistics, 2008), 2, http://bjs.ojp.usdoj.gov/content/pub/pdf/pptmc.pdf (accessed January 18, 2010).

2. Craig Haney and Philip Zimbardo, "The Past and Future of U.S. Prison Policy Twenty-Five Years after the Stanford Experiment," *American Psychologist* 53, no. 7 (1998): 716, http://proxychi.baremetal.com/csdp.org/research/haney_apa.pdf (accessed April 13, 2010).

3. Susan Phillips and Barbara Bloom, "In Whose Interest? The Impact of Changing Public Policy on Relatives Caring for Children with

Incarcerated Parents," in *Children with Parents in Prison: Child Welfare Policy, Program & Practice Issues*, ed. Cynthia Seymour and Creasie Finney Hairston (Piscataway, NJ: Transaction, 2000), 71.

4. Glaze and Maruschak, "Parents in Prison," 2.

5. Creasie Finney Hairston, "Focus on Children with Incarcerated Parents: An Overview of the Literature," report prepared for the Annie E. Casey Foundation (Baltimore, 2007), 24–25, http://www.aecf.org/SearchResults.aspx?keywords=incarceration&source=topsearch (accessed April 13, 2010); Christina Jose Kampfner, "The Care and Placement of Prisoners' Children," in *Children of Incarcerated Parents*, ed. Katherine Gabel and Denise Johnston (New York: Free Press, 1995), 138.

6. John Hagan and Juleigh Petty Coleman, "Returning Captives of the American War on Drugs: Issues of Community and Family Reentry," *Crime and Delinquency* 47, no. 3 (2001): 352.

7. Millie Harris and Corretta Pettway, "Best Practices Tool Kit: Incarcerated Parents and Parenting," report prepared for the Ohio Institute on Correctional Best Practices at Ohio State University (Columbus).

8. Hairston, "Focus on Children," 14.

9. Denise Johnston, "Effects of Parental Incarceration," in *Children of Incarcerated Parents*, ed. Katherine Gabel and Denise Johnston (New York: Free Press, 1995), 78.

10. Ibid., 80.

11. Veronica Crawford Lynch, "An Exploratory Investigation into the Relationship of Mother-Daughter Attachment and Perceived Maternal Emotional Support to Mental Health Outcomes among Late-Stage Adolescent Female Offenders" (PhD diss., Howard University, 2008), 15.

12. Child Welfare League of America, "Family Reunification," Research 2 Practice Brief (Baltimore: Author, 2002), 5, http://www.cwla.org/programs/r2p/rrnews0203.pdf (Accessed April 13, 2010).

13. Stacey M. Bouchet, "Children and Families with Incarcerated Parents: Exploring Development in the Field and Opportunities for Growth," a report prepared for the Annie E. Casey Foundation (Washington, DC, 2008), 8, http://www.aecf.org/ (accessed April 13, 2010).

14. Ibid.

15. Judith Greene and Kevin Pranis, "Hard Hit: The Growth in the Imprisonment of Women, 1977–2004. Report for the Women's Prison Association. http://www.wpaonline.org/institute/hardhit/part1.htm (accessed April 13, 2010).

16. Christopher J. Mumola, "Incarcerated Parents and Their Children" (Washington, DC: Bureau of Justice Statistics, 2000), 6, http://bjs.ojp.usdoj.gov/index.cfm?ty=pbdetail&iid=981 (accessed April 13, 2010).

17. Lynch, "Exploratory Investigation," 69.

18. Johnston, "Effects of Parental Incarceration," 71.

19. Mumola, "Incarcerated Parents and Their Children."

Chapter 11

A Holistic Approach to the Trauma of Reentry

LONNIE MCLEOD

Over the past twenty years, I've done a great deal of practical work with persons reentering society after serving a prison or jail sentence. I believe returning to life on the outside after serving a prison sentence is a far more complex social process than most churches and individuals realize. Building a better understanding of the challenges that face persons in reentry is essential for the church and all who think critically about its ministry.

Traditionally, those ministering to returning citizens have often focused on providing for what psychologist Abraham Maslow called "primary needs"—food, clothing, and shelter. Although the fulfillment of primary needs is essential, simply meeting these basic requirements does little toward the greater goal of successful reentry that leads to full integration into the community. I use the term *integration* rather than *reintegration*, because many of the people returning from our prisons and jails have never truly participated as adults in what is referred to as "society." Many of these men and women entered prison as young adults after years in the foster care and juvenile justice systems. Most do not have a high level of education, and few were holding steady jobs before their arrests. A large number have produced offspring but never contributed to the welfare of those children in a substantial way. It is also important to note that many persons reentering society from prison were raised in single-parent homes or were brought up by a grandparent as primary caregiver.

This socioeconomic and cultural dislocation from the mainstream community that the returning citizen has experienced contributes to a state of emotional and psychological dysfunction that I call "transitional trauma." This trauma is closely related to *anomie*, a term sociologist Emile Durkheim used to describe the absence of socially accepted norms and values. Put simply, many persons caught in the criminal justice system never gained a clear sense of the ways in which society determines right and wrong, good and evil. Their lifestyles reflect a form of pragmatism that judges the appropriateness of an action based solely on their own desires, often disregarding or oblivious to the ways others are affected by their behavior. (See chapter 3 for more information).

The criminal justice system takes such individuals and confines them for years under the harshest and most rigid standards allowed by our nation. And then these persons are released into a society that offers more freedom than any other on earth. Without a moral compass, the shift from confinement to freedom is traumatic. Additionally, returning citizens face countless barriers and stigmas that make it difficult to assimilate and integrate immediately into mainstream society. Durkeim noted that the state of anomie he studied often led to suicide. In a similar way, this transitional trauma and inability to integrate into meaningful particpation in the social order can lead to a "social suicide" for the returning citizen and the reenactment of criminal lifestyles.

In today's professional jargon concerning prisoner reentry, this inability to integrate into society is attributed to a lack of "pro-social skills." Interestingly, reentry experts agree that the development of pro-social skills is an important component of successful reentry, alongside such staples as housing, employment, substance abuse treatment, and mental health provisions. However, research reveals that most reentry programs emphasize those tangible services—employment, housing, and so on—and give less attention to the dynamics that produce pro-social skills. Even when you ask returning citizens about their needs when coming home from incarceration, those same tangible concerns hold center court, while concern for structures that would foster social skills receive little if any attention. This is not surprising: when people are unaware of the existence and necessity of certain social skills, they are unlikely to seek support for gaining and improving these skills.

Similarly, the trauma of incarceration itself receives significant attention in discussions by those who care about the plight of prisoners and the conditions of correctional facilities. But we have been much slower to recognize the great trauma involved in the rentry process. Trauma is, at its root, an overwhelming fear caused by circumstances that threaten an individual's sense of self-esteem and security. In her work with organizations that serve individuals impacted by trauma, psychiatrist Sandra Bloom notes that responding to the results of exposure to trauma—loss of safety, inability to manage emotions, overwhelming losses, and a paralyzed imagination—requires real engagement by individuals and communities with a secure sense of self and support.[1] While professional intervention may be necessary in some cases, congregations can assist in being present as places of understanding and support. Traumatized individuals need understanding, not judgment—people who can see beyond society's stigma and view returning citizens as human beings who have been wounded by their experiences and in need of healing.

Understanding Transitional Trauma

Inmates released back into society face huge decisions concerning where they will live, how they will be employed, and where they will find friendship and support. While the challenges presented by such major choices seems self-evident, other less significant decisions can prove equally traumatizing. Prison Fellowship executive Pat Nolan is a former elected official who served twenty-five months in a federal correctional institution for accepting an illegal campaign contribution. After his release from prison, a group of friends took Nolan to a deli for lunch. His friends ordered. Nolan's own description of what happened next proves instructive:

> I kept poring over the menu. My eyes raced over the columns of choices. I knew that I was supposed to order, but the number of options overwhelmed me. My friends sat in embarrassed silence. I was paralyzed. The waiter looked at me impatiently. I began to panic. I was mortified that I wasn't able to do such a simple thing as order lunch. Finally, in desperation I ordered the next item my eyes landed on, a turkey sandwich. I didn't even want it, but at least it put an end to this embarrassing incident.[2]

After having no choice about his food during his two years in prison, Nolan says he was left in a panic when faced with this choice. How much more of a struggle faces people who have served more time, who have less educational and professional background, and who had minimal social supports prior to incarceration. In his book *When Prisoners Return* (Prison Fellowship, 2004), Nolan gives an important list of needs that people returning from prison require and in which congregations can participate. They include the need for a changed heart and mind, loving mentors, a safe place to live, a good job, access to health care, freedom from addiction, repair of harm done by crime, and participation in improving conditions in the community.[3] But it is instructive that many who have heard Nolan speak recall his testimony concerning the traumatic experience in the deli and his need for support in a seemingly simple task.

Likewise, at the 2009 meeting of the Christian Association for Prisoner Aftercare, Rhozier "Roach" Brown told of a visit to a restroom at Union Station in Washington, DC, immediately following his release from prison. After using the toilet, Brown stood up and the toilet flushed automatically. "I turned around to see who did that! I kept my fists cocked as I approached the sink, looking over my shoulder for who flushed my toilet. I was going to knock somebody out. When I unballed my fists to wash my hands, the water came on! 'Who did that!' Somebody was going to get knocked out!" Brown laughs at himself now, realizing that while he was away, technological innovation had provided automatic toilets and faucets for public places. But he is clear about what would have helped: "I just needed someone to walk with me and explain what was going on."

Formerly incarcerated persons commonly tell stories of standing and waiting for doors in their homes and other places to open because of their years having to stand before a door and wait for a correctional office to turn the key or for a buzzer to signal the opening of an automatic door. Communities of support can accompany people experiencing the traumatizing changes of reentry. Congregations and their membership networks can be places where fears are processed, events explained, disappointments understood, and choices supported. While it is good for returning citizens to have mentors, such as those supplied by programs funded by the Second Chance Act of 2008, it is even better when they can be part of a healing community.

The Second Chance Act of 2008 provides federal funding for prisoner reentry programs. It awards grants in several categories, including juvenile justice, community and faith-based mentoring, and criminal justice prison reform. For a detailed overview of the impact of this legislation for the faith community, see Linda Mills, "Justice, Mercy and the Land of the Second Chance," in *Prism: America's Alternative Evangelical Voice* (July/August 2010).

I press this community-based response to trauma because a community—in this case a church congregation—can provide a sense of belonging for a person returning from incarceration. But if that congregation does not recognize the trauma, and treats the returning citizen with stigma and disdain, the trauma will only be increased. Dr. Sandra Bloom's work with the Sanctuary model is one leading campaign to help organizations move beyond the tendency to stigmatize and retraumatize and instead offer real ministries of healing and wholeness.

A Systemic Response to Trauma

Returning citizens need a new social group, a new community, a new system into which they can enter as part of their return to society. They have been hurt by systems; they can find healing in a systematic approach to their sense of trauma.

Few would argue that poverty and crime are unrelated, and that both have systemic roots. The failing institutions in poor neighborhoods are evidence of the powerful effect of the lack of a strong social system on the lives of those living in these neighborhoods. Over the years, many programs addressing poverty, crime, and recidivism have been developed, and some have produced measurable results that show their effectiveness. But the overall condition of poverty, crime and recidivism has remained virtually the same. The only way this reality will change is through broad collaboration that builds supportive relationships that supplement the complementary services individual programs provide.

Collaboration is a systemic approach to systemic problems. It involves networks of people and institutions coming together around an issue. Indeed, collaboration enables a holistic approach to reentry, as opposed to treating the returning citizen in light of just one challenge or another. But the leadership of many service organizations is often a primary barrier to collaboration.

Many faith-based and community organizations are led by charismatic visionaries who have founded these minsitries out of their own personal history and have a strong sense of ownership over the organizations they have developed. In addition, a charismatic leader's ego is sometimes inseparably tied to his or her particular organization, making it hard for such organizations to network effectively together. Charismatic leaders can organize people around a mission and vision with passionate oratory and can quickly convince others to become active in a cause. Indeed, the initial stages of many programs flourish because of charismatic visionaries whose personalities and rhetoric bends others to their will. The charismatic leader becomes the embodiment of the cause and leads by eloquence, passion, and emotionalism. But this gift can also be a curse. Charisma cannot be duplicated and replicated, and an organization's mission often soon falls apart when the founder is no longer present. Since such organizations often develop out of the leaders' experiential and personal development, there is no model or blueprint left behind for others to follow. Therefore, many viable and effective organizations and programs ceased to exist after the departure of a leader. Others continue to work in a vacuum, unable to provide a full range of support because they are disconnected from other services that could help provide a fully developed holistic approach.

A fragmented approach to service delivery cannot produce wholeness. Neither can a theology that denies the efficacy of God working through other organizations and programs to produce wholeness. "One plants, one waters, but God gives the increase" (see 1 Corinthians 3:7) works only when we trust that God works through a variety of people with differing gifts and talents. Just as planters must trust waterers, housing providers must trust job trainers, community groups must trust religious organizations, those who provide social services must trust those who provide relationships and nurture, and so on. The personal care expressed in a community of believers who accompany an individual through moments of trauma supplements direct services of housing, job training, or substance abuse treatment that address specific situations that produce trauma.

Reentry: A Journey Not a Destination

To effectively address the trauma of reentry, all parties involved—returning citizens, their families, and their congregations and communities—must acknowledge that reentry is a journey, not a destination. This was made clear at Sing Sing prison, where inmates were working toward a master's of professional studies degree through a program sponsored by New York Theological Seminary. Inmates in a Hebrew Bible class delved eagerly into the exodus story because of its emphasis on deliverance and its focus on the Promised Land. Many saw a connection between this biblical narrative and their own sense of the inmate's journey. Prison clearly found representation in the bondage of Egypt, while reentry became associated with the Promised Land.

At the same time, however, course participants had to come to grips with the fact that the exodus narrative did not move directly from Egypt to Canaan; rather, the experience of deliverance from bondage is followed by the wilderness. Wandering and wondering, considering the seeming security of Egypt to be superior to the march into the unknown, the Israelites stumbled and struggled with unbelief, doubt, and insecurity during their wilderness journey. In fact, virtually none of those who experienced the initial deliverance from Egypt actually set foot in the Promised Land. The student inmates saw similar track records for those they knew who had been released from prison only to find that their expected step into the Promised Land was really a trek into the wilderness.

Those who were arrested again and returned to prison after release had not considered the interim—the journey through the wilderness. What society judged to be criminal incorrigibility and the propensity to recidivate, the students of the exodus recognized as the inability to appropriately gauge the nature of reentry. They did not blame the victim; rather, they offered that successful passage through the trauma of reentry required two things: (1) that those leaving prison recognize that their release was to the wilderness, not the Promised Land, and (2) that returning citizens be surrounded by a network of support from a variety of sources (collaboration) as they make the transition back into society.

These conversations among student inmates gave birth to the idea for the Exodus Transitional Community. They describe the process thus:

> The biblical name "Exodus" serves as a perfect metaphor for how we view the reentry process. In the Bible, when the Hebrews fled slavery in Egypt, many thought that their release from bondage was the end of their difficult journey. Yet instead of finding themselves in the land of milk and honey, they had to wander through the desert for 40 years before reaching the Promised Land. Likewise, many incarcerated individuals believe that once they leave their state of bondage, their problems are over. Yet in truth, like the ancient Hebrews, they will more likely be wandering in their own wilderness—struggling with financial, family, and social issues—before they reach the promised land of full reintegration into mainstream society. The Exodus Model is designed to provide the support formerly incarcerated individuals need to work through their own wilderness.[4]

Central to the Exodus approach is a six-page contract that each returning citizen develops to delineate his or her goals and plans in six specific areas: employment, education, spirituality, family, health/physical fitness, and community service. Each returning citizen is also linked with an Exodus coach who commits to a year of support while the returning citizen exercises the terms of the contract. By meting out the tasks of reentry in incremental steps, measuring progress, and achieving success in specific accomplishments, returning citizens gain "a vision of a brighter future," and seeing that "achieving the life they want is within their control...if they are willing to do the necessary work for it."[5]

The Exodus Transitional Community, under the direction of Julio Medina, has received national attention for its ability to work collaboratively with a number of organizations, agencies, and congregations in order to provide significant support for persons returning from incarceration. The use of the Exodus Contract assures that returning citizens take responsibility for their own pathway through the wilderness, while also benefiting from the support and partnership of others. This support includes helping returning citizens come to grips with notions of accountability and responsibility. Their individual reformation and transformation of character remains one of the largest challenges of the wilderness experience. Exodus places a great deal of emphasis on the right blend of integrity and character among its staff, as should any ministry that seeks to work with returning citizens and their families. Even the best model will not produce the desired outcome if staff are not adequately trained and motivated; whereas a less comprehensive approach may still bring some satisfactory results if the people involved are well prepared, compassionate, and capable.

One of the strengths of the Exodus Transitional Community is the way its workers understand themselves as a community of servants. Eschewing the traditional professional designation of "staff," they choose the term *community* to reflect the strength of relationships among the professionals working in the ministry and the sense of connection they build with returning citizens. Since many of those who work at Exodus are themselves men and women who have served time, they engage empathically with those who turn to them in the reentry process.

Of course, such empathic listening can be performed in any number of relational contexts—and certainly should become part of the approach of any church caring for its own. Exodus Transitional Community, like other organizations and ministries that understand the trauma of reentry, knows that human beings naturally resist change, yet change must take place both in the life of the reentering citizen and those around her or him, for the transition to be successful. It is time for our congregations to become the kind of caring communities that can respond holistically to returning citizens, supporting them as they journey through the wilderness of transition toward the promise of healing and wholeness for themselves and their communities.

▪ NOTES ▪

1. Dr. Bloom's work on trauma is easily accessible through her Sanctuary Model of caregiving at www.santuaryweb.com.

2. See "The Testimony of Pat Nolan, President of Justice Fellowship, Prison Fellowship Ministries," on page 43 of "Offender Reentry: What Is Needed to Provide Criminal Offenders with a Second Chance?" Hearing before the Subcommittee on Crime, Terrorism and Homeland Security of the Committee on the Judiciary, House of Representatives 109th Congress, First Session, November 9, 2005.

3. Authored by Nolan with foreward by Chuck Colson, *When Prisoners Return: Why We Should Care and How You and Your Church Can Help* (Prison Fellowship, 2004), offers a timely rationale, biblical mandate, and practical solutions for ministry with persons returning from incarceration.

4. See the website of the Exodus Transitional Community at www .etcny.org.

5. Ibid.

Chapter 12

A Letter to African American Churches Concerning the Saints Coming Home from Prison

MADELINE McCLENNEY-SADLER

What would the apostle Paul do if he heard about the mistreatment of brothers and sisters who return to our congregations and communities after being released from prison? I think we know exactly what Paul would do: Paul would write a letter!

I write this letter to the contemporary church using the hybrid style of a Pauline epistle and scholarly article. According to this viewpoint, Jesus was among us only a few years ago, emancipation was only a few days ago, and the appointed time to act for God's reign is now.

Madeline, a servant of Jesus Christ, called to be an apostle, set apart for the gospel of God, which he promised beforehand through his prophets in the Holy Scriptures, the gospel concerning his Son, Jesus Christ our Lord, through whom we have received deliverance from cruel and oppressive slave masters who once sold us on the auction block like cattle, lynched us for defending our families, and raped us only to enslave our shared offspring. Despite our legal emancipation by God's command and the 13th Amendment of the U.S. Constitution, prison plantations across the nation have continued to hold generation after generation of our sons and daughters in unjust bondage to this day.

To all God's beloved in the United States and the African diaspora, who are called to be saints and to work for the good of all, including those returning home from prison to face obstacle upon obstacle while rebuilding a new life:

Grace to you and peace from God our Father and the Lord Jesus Christ.

First, I thank my God through Jesus Christ for all of you because your faith is proclaimed throughout the world. From South Africa to Palestine, from Ireland to China our brothers and sisters in Christ find courage because of your faith. They sing our song, "We Shall Overcome," and they march in public squares for deliverance from oppressive hands in their own lands. Our witness to a God who delivers from oppression and saves us from ourselves has been an inspiration to believers and nonbelievers worldwide. Yet despite everything our God has taught us about fairness and impartiality, there is a troubling practice reported among our churches. It grieves me to have to address it, but we must root out every evil practice so that we might present ourselves before our God with clean hands.

It is said that some members of the body are mistreating the saints coming home from prison. It is reported that measures have been taken to limit the access of saints with criminal records to full participation in the body of Christ. It is further reported that members of the body fear the saints who have been incarcerated and do not want to minister to them. It is said that these saints have been told they are underdressed for church. Equally disturbing are the descriptions of the "evil eye" many have experienced upon entering the church for the first time after release from prison. In many of our congregations, returning citizens are pulled aside and scolded for failing to know what they were never taught.

Strive with me, beloved, and we shall address these issues and pursue a remedy. We shall open our hearts to the convicting power of the Holy Spirit and pursue a more holy union together, as one body in Christ. The remedy to be presented will be informed by the teachings of our Lord and Savior Jesus Christ, and his apostles, his saints, and his martyrs. Let us begin by exorcising our own demons—the three most persistent obstacles to treating returning citizens as welcomed saints. They are *fear, denial,* and *crack theology.* Let us first consider fear.

Fear

The root of the fear about returning citizens is a fear of contamination. Many in the body of Christ are afraid the church will be soiled, stained, or dirtied by what we assume returning citizens might bring into the congregation. They worry that something dirty will invade the clean space that has been set aside for God. They are concerned about the congregation's purity. Let us consider two specific examples of this fear.

First, some members of the body of Christ fear that people coming home from prison will contaminate them by bringing new or forbidden styles of dress into the congregation. In order to stop this threat of contamination, some churches are unconsciously using a tactic common to human cultures around the world yet foreign to what we have received in our Holy Scriptures. In my last letter to you, I described this "strategy of exclusion"[1] as being like a "purity trial" or a modern-day witch hunt.[2] It has four phases:

1. An accusation of minor moral weakness is made. For example: "I think he has been in trouble with the law."

2. The accusation progresses to full imputation of filthy living: "He looks like he's still using drugs; I bet he has a record."

3. The individual is accused of causing *insidious harm* so severe that he or she is classed as a public nuisance by consensus of the congregation or its authorities: "I'm offended by the way he comes to church in jeans, tattoos, and dreadlocks."

4. Actions are taken to prevent further damage or to exorcise the target from the congregation: "We'll have to get the pastor or deacon board to pull him aside. He can't sing in the choir like that."

We must eliminate these tactics from the Lord's house! Do you not remember what Jesus said? "Woe to you scribes and Pharisees, hypocrites! For you clean the outside of the cup and of the plate, but inside they are full of greed and self-indulgence. You blind Pharisee! First clean the inside of the cup, so that the outside also may become clean. Woe to you scribes and Pharisees, hypocrites! For you are like whitewashed tombs, which on the outside look beautiful, but inside they are full of the bones of the dead and of all kinds of filth. So you also on the outside look righteous to others, but inside you are full of hypocrisy and lawlessness" (Matthew 23:25-28).

Jesus also said, "Do not judge by appearances, but judge with right judgment" (John 7:24). I am speaking the truth in Christ—I am not lying; my conscience confirms it by the Holy Spirit, anyone who judges another based on outward appearance—whether baggy pants, cleavage, short skirts, jeans, earrings, tattoos or dreadlocks—does not judge with right judgment and is in danger of the fiery furnace. The church is already contaminated by middle-class codes of conduct. The slave masters of old ripped off our native attire and taught us how to dress to please them. Shall we repeat their error in our own community? Shall we disregard the image of God in a recovering gang-banger and make him win the approval of new masters? Shall we be intimidated because a teenage girl wears a party dress to church, when it is the only dress she owns? Are our minds so debased that the slightest hint of sexual beauty is a threat to worship? Have we forgotten that women were lynched for showing their ankles in this country years ago? Have we forgotten that women are being burned alive for showing their faces in Afghanistan? The source of the evil has never been with ankles, faces, legs, or thighs. The source of the evil is in our minds.

Beloved, we must be transformed by the renewing of our minds. We can overcome this obsession with appearances. We can be free to love. We can be free to welcome any person in any form with open arms. If he has five earrings, fingernail polish, and a nose ring, we can love him! If she has a skirt up to her midriff and cleavage that would make a lingerie model blush, we can make her feel welcomed. We can continue to socialize our youth and provide *suggestions* to adults *who request our advice* about how to dress for success in the business world. Yet we must give up unsolicited individual censorship.

Jesus never addressed attire in his recorded ministry. "Sunday best" may be a ritual worth preserving in some situations, but not through pharisaic legalism or at the expense of an invitation to "Come as you are" to see God. The only instruction regarding attire in the New Testament is to focus on good works not attire (1 Timothy 2:10), and to treat people we might regard as poorly dressed the same as everyone else (James 2:1-9). We must not teach the standards of the world or our own personal preferences as if they are biblical standards. The Spirit of the Lord is reminding the church that these attitudes about dress and decorum are cultural, not religious; based on one particular moment in time, not eternal revelation; geographically determined, not globally fixed; historically determined, not scripturally stamped. I, Madeline, hear the Lord saying to the churches:

They condemn those whom I did not condemn. They repel those whom I have not repelled. I created the bodies of my children. In all their glorious diversity and creative adornment, I love them so much! How colorful is the variety of their attire? How different are the things that they purpose in their hearts when they get dressed to see me. O Preacher, are your attitudes about dress deeply personal and spiritual? So are theirs! Do not treat them as whores and pimps or ignorant fools. Do not put words in my mouth. I sent them naked into the world. Naked they may come to see me. Come and worship me. Come as you are. I will change what I want to change. Children of Moses, descendants of African slaves, preach and teach by my council. Fear not! Let me adjust the heart of anyone whose motives are unclean—including you! Be guided not by corporate standards or by department stores, but by my Spirit! I am working on more than what the world desires. A suit and tie mean nothing to me. A longer hem is a waste of natural materials. My followers in Africa and India are bare breasted, and they worship me just fine! Who asked this of you? My Spirit is at work in each life. Keep unclean hands off! Do you know how many of my servants I had to use to get each of them into my house? If you cause them to run away, I could lose them forever. If you welcome them, I can transform them, just as I transformed you. If you reject them, I will reject you! says the Lord.

But there is a second way in which fear is plaguing our churches. You say, "But what if a returning citizen contaminates the congregation by committing a new crime against one of the brothers or sisters in the church?" Did not the disciple tell us, "Perfect love casts out fear?" Have we not been warned that fear is a ravenous adversary that seeks to destroy and bring death to us all? Our fears are a plot against the resurrecting power of Jesus to deliver a returning citizen. Our fears are a conspiracy against the transformative power of the Holy Spirit.

How is it that so many shepherds and disciples of our Lord and Savior Jesus Christ want to feed his sheep only in the perceived safety of the prison? Even our government and the prison system itself are crying out for Christians to embrace people when they return home, rather than just singing hymns and reading the Bible to them when they are locked up. Our fears are contaminating everything we touch, and only those saints who remain fearless and strong in the Lord, who rely on the gifts of the Spirit, will be effective in ministry to saints coming home or anyone else for that matter.

If we were really concerned about congregational safety, we would preach more stridently against the physical, sexual, and emotional abuse of women, children, and those least capable of defending themselves. If we were really concerned about safety, we would educate church members and make them streetwise. If we were really concerned about safety, we would complete background checks on anyone coming in contact with children and any who have authority over others—from the pulpit to the pew.

I wish I could tell you that those who are injured, who have injured others, and have gone to prison, will never injure again. I wish I could tell you living for Christ is risk-free. I cannot. But, I *can* tell you that I have been serving with people who were homeless and people in prison for more than twenty years, and the people who have injured me most were church people. They should be afraid of us! Our Savior said, "For those who want to save their life will lose it, and those who lose their life for my sake will save it" (Luke 9:24). If we remain fearful and silent, while others are taken to the slaughter, God will judge us severely (Proverbs 24:10-12).

Do not spend your energy worrying about death, sisters and brothers in Christ. Instead, live out the Lord's Prayer to make God's kingdom "on earth as it is in heaven." Until you complete your mission, whether at age nine or ninety, press on! Be assured, Beloved, the vast majority of our brothers and sisters coming home from prison are not indiscriminately violent. Eighty percent were incarcerated for nonviolent charges. Overcome your fear of death and serve the Lord. Make peace with God, and trust that you are in the Lord's hands. Then open the gates of the church and serve as wisely as serpents but fearlessly! Do not force future generations of Christians to write that we did not show up to serve the kingdom because we were afraid we would get hurt.

Denial

The second demon that prevents us from serving formerly incarcerated persons and their families is denial. Denial is resistance to truth. It is the by-product of fear, fatigue, lack of information, and diminishing hope. Beloved, I once heard a white sister in ministry with returning citizens tell a group of black church members at a black church, "I'm so glad to see you here, because I don't see you coming out to help your own after being released from prison." Wow, did that sting. She was both right and wrong. She was right in saying we need to show up. Yet she was wrong to suggest we were not already doing so. In fact, we are showing up and ministering on many different fronts. However, more of us need to show up to stop this treachery.

Beloved, I know we have been fighting an uphill battle. I am not placing blame. I know you are worn out. God's brown people are under attack by ill-conceived public policy, predatory lending practices, and political backlash that follows every forward step taken in this country. Add the problems of teen fatherhood, failing schools, sexism, racism, and classism, and we can barely carry the weight. It is easy to lose hope. The 30 percent of us who are active in the church cannot meet all these needs. We certainly cannot meet these challenges if we are in denial about how badly we are actually doing as a community. If we accept the truth, if we step back so others can get involved, and if we fulfill the Great

Commission and bring others (no matter who they are) to our houses of worship to be embraced by the Light of the World, then our troops will increase.

Are you ready for the truth? I will tell you the truth. We are losing. Fellow sojourners, it is exceedingly clear that the part of the village inhabited by God's brown people is being decimated. Look at the scoreboard. The statistics do not lie. I hear the prophet Jeremiah's voice echoing across the centuries, "Hear, O women, the word of the Lord, and let your ears receive the word of his mouth; teach to your daughters a dirge, and each to her neighbor a lament. 'Death has come up into our windows, it has entered our palaces, to cut off the children from the streets and the young men from the squares'" (Jeremiah 9:20-21). The forces of death impersonate lady justice and strike the gavel to send our offspring from the classroom to urine-stained cells. Unquenchable *premature* death loves to consume that which is poor, black, and brown. Rise up, women of the church; save the children you adore. You are the extension cords for power and life.[3] They are yours either by biology or by community affinity.

Rise up, also, you men of the church, the remnant whom God has chosen to spare. You were not spared because you are beautiful brown men—although you are indeed! You were spared to be vessels of God's redemptive power. As vessels of God's power, do not do what the sexist ones do and embrace rhetoric that demonizes God's black daughters. You have heard it said, "Black women are taking all the jobs." This is not a competition, beloved. Never forget how black women shielded you on the plantation and later in the workplace. She has never been your opponent. The sexes are not meant for battle but for loving partnerships with Christ only as the head.[4] Remember that every younger woman is your daughter either by birth or social network. Every older woman is your sister or mother. Black women are fighting against two hell-inspired idolatries: white supremacy and male supremacy. Only if you join in both battles can we ascend together and overcome our decimation. Become a good womanist theologian and fight for the survival of the entire black family: men, women, girls, and boys alike.[5] Put your focus where your passion is, yet do not compete—collaborate!

Disciple of our Lord, Carl Upchurch, a self-proclaimed former "drug dealer" and "thug," urged us to remember the brutal fact that too many of our children are "convicted in the womb." In his own letter to the saints, Upchurch called us to move beyond our denial:

> The fundamental goodness of humankind that many of us take for granted has been overshadowed by desolation: by substandard living conditions: multigenerational poverty; rampant drug use and abuse; open street drug sales; inadequately clothed children; hazardous playing areas; disproportionate numbers of high school dropouts and teen mothers [and fathers]; local retail price gouging; gross idleness, particularly on the part of teens; and health hazards caused by maggots, flies, dead animals and garbage that litter the streets. Where is our outrage?[6]

The outrage is muffled, especially among parts of the body that are captive to a third demon...

Crack Theology

Brothers and sisters, crack theology is God-talk that gets you on an emotional high. This false God-talk is the third obstacle to creating a welcoming community. With crack theology, the drug of choice is the promise of greater wealth and a life with virtually no pain.

It's time to get off the pipe. Come back, brother and sister. The Lord our God is merciful. God is slow to anger. Recovery is yours. Pursuit of the "things" of this world is bankrupt.

Keep sight of the faith. Come back, preacher. Restore balance to your sermons about abundance.

Look at what is happening. People coming home from prison are not being fully served. They return to churches whose shepherds preach the messages of greed-based business schools, commercials, movies, boardrooms, and workplaces. All over the country, too many of the Lord's servants are pushing the "prosperity gospel."

Be wary of these wolves in shepherds' clothing that pimp and prostitute you for the dime bag they call a tithe. Sojourners, the purpose of the tithe is to enable the church to care for its servant-leaders, as well as the poor, the widow, the orphan, and in our day, the returning citizen (Deuteronomy 14:29). Yet crack theology teaches that the left out will be saved by the "gospel of prosperity." Like cocaine and crack, this false gospel promises an easy fix. It proposes that the accumulation of wealth and material goods is morally neutral and necessary for human happiness.[7] The prosperity gospel promises that the Christian faith, when invested properly, will yield a good economic return.[8] It teaches that to get money for *yourself* you have to give money.

The prosperity gospel is crack to the church. God is ready to deliver the saints from this high. Only then will we be able to fully serve his creation and fulfill his purposes.

Beloved, in a spirit of love, gently correct anyone addicted to crack theology, and be careful that you yourself are not tempted. When a brother or sister returns home from prison or gets out of the drug game, he or she should not have to face another pusher in the church or pulpit. Church crack is so widespread you can get it on any television station. All of us must be on guard. It creeps into churches that do not sell it. It is very difficult to distinguish between church crack and the biblical teaching that promises abundant life.

Be wary of any formula that promises you that God will bring you financial prosperity if you simply follow steps a, b, and c. When God is *obliged* to act on demand, the result is superstition.[9] Remember, prosperity is our birthright, but suffering is our inheritance. We have inherited the suffering of Christ. We are here in this lifetime to continue the redemptive work of Christ who urges each of us to "take up your cross and follow me." Though riches may come to you so that you may bless others, your reward for following Christ is not riches, beloved. It is a cross. Do not get it twisted.

A saint once said, "The fact remains: private happiness can exist as a permanent condition of public suffering only if it is based on delusion."[10] Anyone who pursues personal happiness when so much of the world is suffering is deluded. Mass incarceration is destroying God's creation. If you are called to a different type of ministry, pursue that calling with vigor. Yet do not become an obstacle to the pastor or disciples who are working to create a welcoming house of worship and healing for returning citizens. Resist crack theology that encourages you to avoid the truth.

Beloved, our ship is sinking like the *Titanic*. Anyone traveling in first class must unlock the gates for those in third class and share the life rafts. Support the rescue—or sink with those who are fearful, in denial, or on church crack.

All Hands On Deck

When we resist the demons of fear, denial and crack theology, we begin the rescue effort. Here are five steps congregations can take to become true houses of welcome for the saints coming home from prison and for all of God's least, lost, and left out:

1. Adopt as a congregation a "welcoming church credo," and post it in *several* highly visible locations within your church building. Also, consider publishing it regularly in the church newsletter, bulletins, and announcements, and including it in your opening prayers. The written statement will serve as a

centering credo for the whole community. It will help counter acts of individual unfriendliness. Use the following text as a model, adjusting it as needed:

> ABC Church is committed to becoming one of the most welcoming and friendly churches in God's creation. We mean it when we say, "Come as you are!" God looks on the inside not the outside. If you have been in any form of bondage and you are making an exodus from prison, drug addiction, prostitution, an abusive relationship, or a mental or physical illness, you can find rest and peace here. Welcome to ABC Church.

2. In preparation for creating a more welcoming church, offer instruction on the following Bible passages. While we often fall into the trap of focusing on the hearts of others, these passages speak to deliverance and self-examination. They are particularly relevant for churches reaching out to returning citizens. Additionally, implement an educational campaign to help the entire congregation grasp the issues related to the mass incarceration of the African American community.[11]

Lamentations 3:34-36: God sees the prisoners.
Luke 4:18: Jesus came to set the captives free.
Hebrew 13:3-4: Remember those in prison.
Matthew 23: Avoid hypocrisy.
John 7:24: Judge not by appearances.
Acts 5:17-42: God opens prison doors.
James 2:1-27: Treat those without wealth in the church fairly.
Philippians 2:1-15: Regard others as better than self.

3. Each year, observe an "Atonement Sunday," on the Sunday after Yom Kippur,[12] a day for all those who are not incarcerated to reflect on how we have contributed to the problem of mass incarceration. Each of us has contributed to the mass incarceration of our youth and young adults in one way or

another, whether it is by abusing our authority over children (70 percent of inmates were abused as children), by failing to speak out against mass incarceration and inadequate educational systems, by refusing to be peacemakers, and/or by refusing to seek reconciliation with those in our own families and communities whom we have victimized or injured. Use this occasion to have an altar call for people who have been incarcerated or have been victims of crime, the families of both, and loved ones left behind.

4. Partner with other churches and community-based organizations to train laypeople to serve as life coaches and mentors for formerly incarcerated persons and their families in a church-based reentry ministry. If this is a new ministry for your church, one great tool for practical assistance is *What Shall We Then Do? A Family Freedom Kit for Creating Healing Communities*. This resource is designed to assist local churches in serving its members who are impacted by mass incarceration. This and other resources can be obtained at no charge by going to www.exodusfoundation.org and visiting the Pastor's Study, or from www.healingcommunities.org.

5. Avoid any preaching that celebrates the old plantation practices of whipping and beating children. The vast majority of those who are incarcerated were physically or sexually abused as children. Our youth know unreserved corporal punishment. They are reacting against those memories today, or repeating them in street organizations. We win the hearts of youth and formerly abused adults coming from prison by demonstrating the discipline of unreserved love. A switch, telephone cord, or dehumanizing smack in the face were part of what led many young people to the streets in the first place. Instead of preaching about picking up a bat to discipline a child, encourage parents to pick up a bat and glove, go to the mound, and spend time with their kids.

And finally, beloved, wherever there is victimization, do not silence its cry. Wherever there is injury, do not cover it up. Wherever there is violence, do not look away. You are God's healing community.[13] Wherever justice is lacking for the victim or the transgressor, create it. Think no longer in terms of criminal justice that punishes, maims, and imprisons. Think in terms of restorative justice that atones, rebuilds, and renews.

May the God who abolished slavery *de jure* (by law) work in you to abolish slavery *de facto* (in reality). Remember that we are all kin. Welcome with joy the saints returning home from prison as members of the household of faith. Never forget that those who have yet to receive Christ are like the murderer Saul before he became Paul—saints in the making. It was Paul who wrote two-thirds of the New Testament. It was a convicted criminal called Jesus who died to save people with a record. Remember, beloved, we all have a record with the Most High.

One thing more, prepare a guest room for me, for I am hoping through your prayers to visit with you. My fellow servants of Exodus Foundation.org send greetings. The grace of the Lord Jesus Christ be with your spirit.

▪ NOTES ▪

1. Mary Douglas, "Witchcraft and Leprosy: Two Strategies of Exclusion" (Man 1991) NS 26:723–36.

2. Madeline McClenney-Sadler, "Cry Witch: The Embers Still Burn," in *Pregnant Passion: Gender, Sex, and Violence in the Bible* Semeia Studies 44 (Herndon, VA: Brill Academics, 2003), 117–41.

3. "The varieties of situations black women confront in the many denominations of the Sanctified Church point to the importance of black women to any endeavor of significance in the black community." Cheryl Townsend Gilkes, *If It Wasn't for the Women* (Mary Knoll, NY: Orbis, 2001), 90.

4. Rodney Sadler Jr. "Resurrection Remix: Strengthening the Family, Ephesians 5:21-33 and 6:1-9." The African-American Pulpit Lectionary Archives. Internet Resource, April 6, 2008, (http://theafricanamerican lectionary.org/PopupLectionaryReading.asp?LRID=20).

5. See *Katie's Canon: Womanism and the Soul of the Black Community* (Continuum, 1995); Cheryl Sanders, *Living the Intersection: Womanism and Afrocentrism in Theology* (Minneapolis: Augsburg, 1995); Kelly Brown Douglas, *The Black Christ* (Mary Knoll, NY: Orbis, 1994); Evelyn Brooks Higganbotham, *Righteous Discontent* (Cambridge: Harvard University Press, 1993); Marcia Riggs, *Can I Get a Witness* (Mary Knoll, NY:

Orbis, 1997); Cheryl Kirk-Duggan and Tina Pippin eds. *Mother Goose, Mother Jones, Mommie Dearest: Biblical Mothers and Their Children* (Atlanta: Society of Biblical Literature, 2009).

6. Carl Upchurch, *Convicted in the Womb: One Man's Journey from Prisoner to Peacemaker* (New York: Bantam, 1996), 217.

7. Robert M. Franklin, *Crisis in the Village: Restoring Hope in African-American Communities* (Minneapolis: Fortress, 2007), 117.

8. Ibid., 118.

9. Gerald G. May, *Will and Spirit: A Contemplative Psychology* (New York: Harper One, 1982), 34.

10. Ibid., 15.

11. Helpful websites for resources include www.exodusfoundation.org; www.21cf.org; www.soros.org; www.aecf.org; www.reentry.gov; www.nationalreentryresourcecenter.org; and www.reentryresources.ncjrs.gov.

12. Please contact Exodus Foundation.org at 704-947-9090 for liturgical aids.

13. Please visit www.healingcommunitiesusa.org to learn about becoming a healing community for victims of crime, people returning from prison, and the families of both.

Chapter 13

The Ministry of the Prison Chaplain

MICHAEL R. SMITH SR.

T he prison chaplain is a unique person called to a unique ministry. I have had the privilege of serving as a prison chaplain for over twenty years in both state and federal prisons. This ministry has offered me the opportunity to serve inmates, their families, and prison staff. Serving as a chaplain has also afforded me opportunities to speak at local churches, denominational gatherings, and national events around the country. Prison chaplains serve in one of our nation's largest and neediest mission fields. The social impact of crime and incarceration on our African American communities demands that churches support the ministry of these dedicated persons serving in prisons and jails around the country. Let's take a look at the unique ministry of the prison chaplain.

The prison chaplain is an ordained clergyperson called to serve lives impacted by crime and incarceration. The call originates from the Spirit of God and is confirmed through the actions of a local church or denominational body that publicly recognizes the individual for prison chaplaincy through formal licensing and ordination procedures. Persons who serve as chaplains must receive formal ecclesiastical endorsement before being employed. Prison chaplaincy has not traditionally been a ministry pathway for African American pastors, which is one reason there are relatively few African Americans serving as chaplains in state and federal prisons. But given the current incarceration crisis affecting our communities, the African American church must increase its support and advocacy for this critical ministry.

The prison chaplain serves within a correctional facility as a representative of the church. Chaplains are professional clergy persons and full-time paid staff. While specific requirements vary from state to state, most prisons require chaplains to have a master of divinity degree and some formal ministry experience prior to service. Prison policy normally mandates that chaplains remain accountable to and in communication with their ordaining body throughout their chaplaincy service.

As an ordained officer of the church, the chaplain has the authority to carry out all church functions, including preaching, teaching, counseling, baptism, communion, last rites, and marriage. The chaplain also serves as a primary conduit for local churches doing outreach ministry among the prison population and can provide education and special training opportunities within the local church. I regret to say that in my experience local churches do not take advantage of services that a prison chaplain can offer nearly as often as they could. Interaction between churches and chaplains serving at jails and prisons in their local communities must increase if we are to address the crime and incarceration crisis in our communities. One possibility is for local pastors to schedule prison chaplains to share in special services or programs that highlight aspects of crime and incarceration. Chaplains can speak knowledgeably about the real issues local churches need to consider.

The Chaplain's Responsibilities

Within the correctional facility, a chaplain's responsibilities fall in three primary areas. First, the chaplain coordinates all the religious programming in the facility. Prison chaplains ensure that people of all religious traditions have opportunity to practice their respective faiths through study and worship opportunities. Chaplains are responsible to recruit religious leaders from the community to meet the needs of the diverse faith groups if they are not able to meet these needs themselves. Chaplains also have the authority to initiate innovative services and programs to address inmates' specific religious needs. Most chaplains oversee a budget that is used to purchase essential religious items for the various faith groups. As facilitator, the chaplain coordinates all religious observances to ensure the legal protection of inmate religious rights in accordance with the U.S. Constitution and federal law.

Second, the chaplain provides religious expertise to all staff and the community. Within the correctional institution, chaplains are the religious leaders and receive ongoing training in regard to different faith groups in order to provide staff with accurate information when needed. As the religious expert, the prison chaplain is involved in the training of other staff regarding religious practices and issues that arise in daily prison operations. This may include advocacy for the legitimate religious rights of inmates or providing staff with advice when an inmate is making an illegitimate request. The religious expertise of the chaplain is critical in guarding the agency against lawsuits for violating inmates' religious rights while also ensuring the security and orderly running of the prison.

Finally, the chaplain serves as the pastor within the institution. This means chaplains provide pastoral care and presence to both inmates and staff. Pastoral care is extended to every inmate regardless of his or her particular religious background or beliefs. Chaplains also provide pastoral support to staff when appropriate. Prison staff do not always have spiritual support on the outside, and pastoral relationships can develop from their daily interactions with the chaplain. In addition, work schedules may prevent staff from attending local church services, so they may choose to attend worship services within the prison or jail. Chaplains extend pastoral support to both inmates and staff through times of illness, death and dying, family crises, and emotional issues, as well as in situations unique to the prison setting, such as emergency lockdowns.

Pastor to the Prisoner

The chaplain's pastoral role with inmates as well as their families is central to this ministry. Chaplains primarily provide a ministry of presence to inmates. Normally, the chaplain will meet new inmates at an orientation session designed to make new arrivals aware of what religious opportunities are available. The relationship between chaplain and inmate often grows as the inmate attends religious services at the prison chapel. Since the normal ratio is 1 chaplain per every 500 inmates, relationships between chaplains and inmates vary in degree of communication and interaction. Chaplains often develop strong pastoral relationships with inmates who share the same faith tradition. A chaplain's relationships with inmates from other faith traditions are normally cordial. These inmates expect the chaplain to ensure they will have time and space scheduled for their own religious services, and to support them through emergency situations such as deaths, illnesses, hospitalizations, and family crises.

The chaplain interacts with inmate families in two primary ways. First, the chaplain is the designated person family members can call to inquire about their loved one or to see that important family information is passed on to the incarcerated family member. These telephone calls are very important in the chaplain establishing positive and support-ive relationships with families, and are also a conduit for strengthening the chaplain's relationships with inmates who usually do not come to the chapel activities.

Second, chaplains interact with families directly while making their rounds during visitation hours. A chaplain's presence during visitation allows him or her to connect per-sonally with both inmates and their families. Chaplains con-sider it a high honor when inmates invite us to share with their families during visitation. Other roles the chaplain ful-fills with inmates and families include marriage counseling, mentoring, and pastoral support during illness or death.

Opportunities for Churches

Based on my two decades of experience as a prison chaplain, I see tremendous opportunities for the church to make a real difference in the lives of those most affected by crime and in-carceration. Within our law-enforcement, judicial, and cor-rectional systems today, there is a new openness to innovative programs for community collaboration, alternative sentenc-ing, and new forms of in-prison and reentry ministries. Chap-lains can play a key role in educating and training churches in their efforts to respond to crime and incarceration. While there continues to be a need for local churches to provide vol-unteers to assist with worship services within prison, the time is now for in-prison ministries to utilize discipleship-teaching models that address specific needs of inmates, such as parent-ing skills, self-respect, and leadership. Discipleship needs to be taught in ways that are applicable to inmates. Doors are open for churches to become more involved in prerelease programs that help prepare inmates for life on the outside and reentry programs that provide mentorship and support after release. Even the very simple yet oft-neglected act of providing transportation for families to visit inmates incarcerated in geographically remote prisons can be a huge way for churches to help. Imagine how much it would mean for a child to be able to see his or her father or mother on a regular basis.

The key to church involvement in many of these efforts is communication with the local prison chaplain. Here are twelve practical steps that churches can take to respond more faithfully to lives impacted by crime and incarceration:

1. Diligently bear witness to the gospel of Jesus Christ by sharing God's truth with inmates in jails and prisons and returning citizens in our communities.
2. Promote restorative justice and mercy to ensure that these are preserved in our society's law enforcement, judicial, and correctional systems.
3. Preach and teach the value of human life in ways that encourage social stability, decency, and civility.
4. Receive into our care and fellowship persons who have been placed on probation or parole and those recently released from prison.
5. Reach out to embrace, comfort, and aid the families who are victims of crime with healing and reconciliation ministries.
6. Support programs that offer specialized training for prison chaplains as well as parachurch ministries that equip persons called to minister to those affected by crime and incarceration.
7. Intentionally bring a biblical perspective and understanding to issues of crime and incarceration in order to maintain the relationship of justice and mercy in prison ministry.
8. Advocate for full-time or community-supported chaplains in prisons that do not have one.
9. Offer both prayer and financial support for prison ministries that evangelize, disciple, and mentor persons while incarcerated.

10. Promote awareness around issues of crime and incarceration through special worship services, conferences, and other activities that educate and equip the church to make a difference.

11. Speak out prophetically to ensure that religious freedom is legally protected for all people, including those who are incarcerated or under criminal-justice supervision.

12. Communicate through word and deed that every single person is of great value to God, and this includes those who are at risk, those who have broken the law, and those whose lives have been touched by crime. No one is excluded from God's love or beyond redemption, no matter what that person has done.

With more than 2 million people incarcerated in state and federal prisons, we are facing a social crisis that demands a quality response from the African American community. The black church must work along with prison chaplains to make prison outreach and reentry ministries a mission priority. If we fail to do this, the old saying, "Evil left unattended will come back to haunt you" will continue to be a greater reality in our communities.

Chapter 14

Chaplains, Families, and Prison Ministry

ELWOOD GRAY

A s a local pastor and retired prison chaplain with more than four decades of experience, and as the president of the National Coalition of Prison Ministries, I have given a lot of thought to the relationship between chaplaincy ministry and the local church. It's essential for churches seeking to minister in a prison setting to understand the important role of chaplains in working not just with persons who are incarcerated but also with families of inmates. Prison chaplains can also be an important resource for congregations seeking to do important ministry in the prison setting. In addition to networking with churches that provide volunteers for traditional prison ministries such as worship services and Bible studies, chaplains are helping churches embark on new and rewarding approaches to their roles as change agents within the prison and their local community.

Working with Families

Remember those who are in prison, as though you were in prison with them; though who are being tortured, as though you yourselves were being tortured.—HEBREWS 13:3

Most church people tend to think of prison chaplains primarily as pastors to persons who are incarcerated—and this is certainly a critical part of the chaplain's role. But it is essential for the church to understand the role chaplains play in working with families of inmates.

The chaplain is the religious authority designated by the prison or jail administration to interact directly with the families of incarcerated persons. Some of the specific areas of communication include procedures for marriages while a person is in prison and family notifications regarding death (of an inmate or a member of his or her immediate family). The chaplain also provides counseling for both inmates and families facing these situations. Chaplains also provide religious referrals in accordance with the tenets of faith for individual inmates and their families.

As the trained religious leader within the correctional institution, the chaplain advises the warden and prison staff regarding matters of religious affiliation of inmates and their families. The chaplain is also a standing member of the classification committee that provides a structured program for inmates while incarcerated as well as during their transitions back to their communities. In this role, the chaplain helps the committee in considering the impact of religion in the life of the inmate and his or her family.

The chaplain also works with inmate families by explaining to them the importance of maintaining personal and family devotions, as well as practices of meditation and reflection in accordance with one's chosen faith. Chaplains encourage and facilitate dialogue about religious matters between incarcerated persons and their family members, and challenges families to continue supporting the religious life of the returning citizen after he or she is released from custody.

Because the families of inmates do not necessarily share the religious beliefs of the incarcerated person, it is paramount that chaplains make themselves available to inmates for advice and counsel. This pastoral relationship is crucial to the inmate's spiritual well-being.

The basic principles of moral and ethical behavior taught by most faiths have proven to have a positive impact on persons returning home from prisons and jails. Prison chaplains, inmate families, and local churches should come together to support religious programming as an essential component of the quest to help in the rehabilitation of persons affected by the criminal justice system.

Networking with Congregations

The Spirit of the Lord is upon me, because he has anointed me to bring good news to the poor. He has sent me to proclaim release to the captives and recovery of sight to the blind, to let the oppressed go free, to proclaim the year of the Lord's favor.—LUKE 4:18

The chaplain is pivotal in identifying ways in which local congregations can support inmates and returning citizens, as well as their families. Chaplains can offer training and suggestions to churches through workshops, seminars, and other speaking engagements in order to enhance the overall scope of the church's knowledge of inmate-family relationships.

Religious leaders from varied faith groups are essential in this collaboration to use religion as a vehicle to forge a better life for the inmate and his or her family. In pursuing supportive partnerships with local congregations, chaplains can speak with particular inmates about whether they (or their families) have connections to a particular church, mosque, or temple. The chaplain can then establish communication with that congregation or with local leaders of the same faith tradition; in some instances, an open interfaith gathering of local religious leaders might be appropriate. This would offer opportunities for local religious bodies to consider "adopting" an inmate and his or her immediate family.

In such situations, the chaplain, the local congregation, and the inmate (and his or her family) would form a triangle of communication and cooperation. Open sharing of information could include opportunities for the inmate and his or her family to speak about the impact of religion in their lives. After hearing from the inmate, the chaplain can offer suggestions and address questions pertaining to that individual's religious needs. Families are often a crucial part of the rehabilitative process because of their knowledge about the background of the inmate prior to and after his/her incarceration. A strong religious foundation can assist the entire family through the experience of having a loved one in prison and during his or her transition back to the community. When a chaplain has opportunities to speak with both an inmate and his or her family, that chaplain is better able to brief the cooperating congregation on ways to provide effective services to the family—both before and after release. These relationships between chaplain, family, and congregation can also be fostered through phone conversations and written communication.

Facilitating Church Ministries in Prison and after Release

I was naked and you gave me clothing, I was sick and you took care of me, I was in prison and you visited.

—MATTHEW 25:36

Chaplains can also help individuals and congregations find opportunities to minister within the prison system. Those who seek to serve God by volunteering within the penal system are actually fulfilling the biblical mandate found in Scriptures like Isaiah 61:1 and Luke 4:18, as well as the Great Commission of Matthew 28:19-20. The prison system provides an excellent opportunity to share the gospel of Christ's love and forgiveness with people who have often sought to solve their personal problems through criminal actions.

Individuals volunteering within the prison system must be mindful of the fact that such service is a holy "calling" and that they are governed by the policies and procedures of the penal system. There is usually an application process that includes a background check and requires a letter of ecclesiastical recommendation from your church or religious organization. The chaplain will orientate volunteers regarding the standard operating procedures within the prison or jail. In many cases, volunteers are required to attend a series of orientation classes conducted by the institution's office of volunteer services in conjunction with the chaplain. These classes may cover areas such as the history of that particular prison or jail, the various departments within the facility, the layout of the physical structure, security issues affecting the movement of volunteers through the facility and its grounds, and the specific role of the volunteer.

In addition to ministry opportunities that involve entering the prison or jail itself, chaplains can also assist churches in finding other ways to serve those who are incarcerated. One of the most basic and essential ways churches can help is by providing personal hygiene kits for inmates. Kits might include a toothbrush, toothpaste, deodorant, soap, and other similar items placed in a plastic bag along with contact information from the church. You can also consider putting devotional readings in these bags as well. The National Coalition of Prison Ministries sponsors a "Love Kit" program that provides such items to inmates. These products are collected from individuals or groups within the church and are dispensed to both male and female inmates through the chaplain.

Chaplains can also assist churches in establishing a "pen pal ministry" in which church members correspond with individual inmates. These pen pal relationships give incarcerated persons the chance to have written dialogue about religious and other nonconfidential matters with someone on the outside. Letters from the outside can be a lifeline for inmates, decreasing their sense of isolation and helping them establish a sense of community when other relationships have become damaged and are in need of healing.

Churches can also consider providing temporary or permanent housing for persons being released from prison. This ministry is in high demand, and grants from local, state, and federal agencies are often available to help fund such outreach. But the search for resources to provide such a ministry can begin with the members of your congregation. You may have within your membership individuals who could provide housing for a returning citizen.

Another area of needed service is employment for persons returning to the community after incarceration. Your church can offer a series of life skills workshops and/or seminars designed to instruct returning citizens in interview techniques, job searching, or basic computer skills. Business owners within the church may be able to provide a job for a returning citizen, helping that person get a fresh start.

Chaplains can be an important resource enabling churches to reach out to those who are currently incarcerated as well as those returning from prison. As chaplains and churches join together in these ministries, we follow in the Spirit of our Lord who "hears the needy, and does not despise his own that are in bonds" (Psalm 69:33).

Chapter 15

Changing Congregational Culture: The Healing Communities Model

HAROLD DEAN TRULEAR

Throughout this book, we have called on churches not so much to develop new and specialized "prison ministries" as to reorient existing congregational resources toward families and individuals affected by crime, the criminal justice system, and incarceration. The question for each congregation is not so much "Can we start this new ministry?" as it is "How can we take what we already have and do, and mobilize it to better serve this population?" As we suggested in the introduction, another way to view this is to ask, "What would it look like if congregations began responding to incarceration in the same way we respond to hospitalization?" In times of illness and even death, every congregation marshals its resources to care for the individuals and families affected. Jesus mentions our faithful response to both incarceration and illness as two marks of the believing church (Matthew 25:31-46). Why do we view responding to illness as the business of the entire congregation, while outreach to the imprisoned is the responsibility of a specialized, often marginalized, ministry team?

Reentry Ministry:
The Work of the Whole Church

Russell Street Baptist Church in Detroit and Praise and Glory Tabernacle in Philadelphia seem about as different as two congregations could be. Russell Street is a historic Baptist church that has been in ministry for nearly a century. Praise and Glory Tabernacle is a relatively young nondenominational Pentecostal congregation just completing its second decade of worship and service. Russell Street numbers about eight hundred members, while Praise and Glory Tabernacle has yet to crack the century mark. Praise and Glory Tabernacle worships in converted commercial space at the end of an alley and is surround by lots and garages. Russell Street's majestic building features traditional church architecture and rises up in view of anyone traveling the Chrysler Freeway. A typical Sunday worship service at Russell Street includes a diverse population of men, women, and children; seniors and youth; singles and families. The worshipping congregation at Praise and Glory Tabernacle is comprised primarily of young adults, with the largest segment between the ages of twenty and forty. Russell Street's pastor—the first female pastor in its long history—is a national officer in an established denomination. Praise and Glory Tabernacle's pastor exercises apostolic leadership as part of a network of smaller congregations. Yet there is one thing that links these two very different congregations together. While neither of them has a formal program focused on incarcerated persons or returning citizens, both of these churches minister to a significant number or people from both of these populations, as well as to their families. How does this happen?

Both Detroit's Russell Street Baptist and Philadelphia's Praise and Glory Tabernacle see work with prisoners, returning citizens, and their families as an essential part of their ongoing life and work. Such ministry may require special training but not necessarily a special department. Each of these churches employs certain individuals to support and coordinate the work, but the same is true for their music ministries and choirs. Simply put, both congregations see ministry with prisoners, returning citizens, and their families as the work of the congregation itself, and not simply the province of a few trained specialists. They do not have "reentry ministries." They are "reentry churches."

This happens because of each congregation's culture—its sense of corporate identity. Each congregation views itself as a community of reconciliation, redemption, forgiveness, and healing. Their overall ministries reflect a commitment to love and hospitality, and that vision extends to include people returning from incarceration and their families.[1] In each of these churches, the preaching, music, conversations, and testimonies reveal the congregation's full ownership of this ministry (as opposed to it simply being the pastor's vision) and indicate the whole church's solidarity with its members, family, and friends affected by crime and incarceration.

While both congregations work actively with the incarcerated, persons returning from incarceration, and their families, they do so in different ways. Russell Street's ministry is done through its formal participation in an initiative called Healing Communities, complete with training manual, the endorsement of the Progressive National Baptist Convention, and foundation support. Like other churches affiliated with the Healing Communities initiative, Russell Street Baptist uses the phrase "Station of Hope" to reflect its desire to be a place where all can find refuge, strength, and acceptance in moving forward with their lives. Praise and Glory Tabernacle ministers to the same population, but without a formal "ministry initiative." The congregation there sings of "PGT for Life," a play on words that signifies both the length of commitment and the presence of a new quality of living for all who come. At Russell Street, public prayer for congregants with an imprisoned family member is integrated into the pastoral prayer. At Praise and Glory Tabernacle, the bulletin board features announcements about persons facing trial and sentencing and requests for letters of support to their judges.

Both Russell Street and Praise and Glory Tabernacle recognize that in order to truly minister to those impacted by crime and incarceration, they must create a climate of acceptance, openness, and honesty. The culture of churches like these resists the stigmatization of incarceration and offers an atmosphere where true reconciliation and redemption can occur. Persons with criminal records, as well as their families, feel free to share their experiences, struggles, strength, and hope within the congregation, both in public worship and in personal interaction. Neither congregation excuses criminal behavior, but both understand such actions within the general context of sin. As such, they call people to accountability, repentance, and renewal, and offer relationships that foster those values.

The Healing Communities Model

As mentioned earlier, Russell Street uses the Healing Communities model. This approach was developed by the Faith and Families portfolio of the Annie E. Casey Foundation in conjunction with the Social Justice and Prison Ministry Commission of the Progressive National Baptist Convention, along with consultative support from Rev. Addie Richburg of the National Alliance of Faith and Justice.[2]

The Healing Communities handbook, *What Shall We Then Do? A Family Freedom Kit*, is a wonderful resource for congregations seeking to expand their ministry to those impacted by crime. The handbook begins with a story of reconciliation between a church member and the murderer of her only daughter. Showing the depths of the possibility for and reality of reconciliation helps reduce the stigmatization of crime and incarceration, and assists congregations in moving toward a posture of reconciliation and healing. Many churches find that discussion of the opening story from the handbook provides opportunities to consider how the historic Christian values of forgiveness, redemption, and reconciliation can be applied to ministry with returning citizens and their families. Each of these values has a relational component; that is, they all involve interaction between persons. Congregations can place inmates, returning citizens, and their families in relationships of support, both formal and informal, that contribute significantly to their sense of belonging to the congregation. For those returning from incarceration, this social support is critical as they seek reintegration into society as a whole.

Healing Communities reject the stigma and shame associated with incarceration and seek to provide social networks that help returning citizens and their families remain connected to the church and neighborhood. The goal is to restore to the community those who have left it. This has led Healing Communities to new language and understandings regarding persons affected by incarceration. Instead of terms like *ex-offender*, *ex-con*, and *ex-felon*, Healing Communities speak of those who have been incarcerated as "returning citizens," challenging the tendency to identify persons in terms of their past, especially a painful part of that past.

The focus on forgiveness, redemption, and reconciliation is central to the Healing Communities model. *Forgiveness* requires "thinking differently" about an offense. Forgiving does not mean forgetting an offense has occurred; rather, it points to the need to receive the offender in spite of the offense, and not define an individual simply or primarily in terms of the offense. Rather than "forgive and forget," the congregational maxim is "forgive and remember differently"—remember that the offender is not defined by the offense and, properly repentant, is capable of living a truly transformed life in spite of his or her past. True forgiveness, as a relational transaction, also calls for offenders to acknowledge their responsibility for their behavior. But such acknowledgment is not a prerequisite for the offer of forgiveness—often it follows a community's sincere desire to forgive.

The word *redemption* draws on the Christian tradition of restoring or "bringing back" what was originally a part of something greater. In this case, the congregations, neighborhoods, and families to which persons return are the "greater thing." Some refer to this process as "restorative justice."[3] This recognizes that while persons returning from incarceration must take responsibility for their decision-making processes upon return to the community, the church and community are also active agents in the restoration process. The congregation and community "pay the price" of mobilizing their resources of care, forgiveness, and support to those who return. The congregation becomes intentional about its role in restoration, creating a sense of welcome and hope for the formerly incarcerated and their families.

Finally, *reconciliation* refers to the reconfiguring of relationships that is a result of the redemptive process. Those who have been incarcerated have committed acts that have brought harm to their neighborhoods, friends, and loved ones, whether intentionally or not. Violent and property offenses bring pain to neighbors. Domestic violence brings clear harm to loved ones. Incarceration brings a separation that can and does strain, fracture, and even sever connections among family members as well as the wider community. Redemptive processes involve the restoring of right relationships among all parties concerned—offender, victim, family members, and the wider community. All are stakeholders in the reestablishment of meaningful relationships that sustain not only the person formerly incarcerated but also those who have been victimized, either directly or indirectly, by that person's actions.

The outgrowth of this process is healing and wholeness—not only for the person returning from incarceration, but also for the entire community of reception and redemption. Successful integration comes not simply when people are given access to services, or even when the services are implemented successfully, but with the wholeness that comes when the community welcomes the returning citizen as one of their own and that individual has accepted the forgiveness inherent in such reception and incorporated it in a new identity structure characterized by increased self-worth and a sense of belonging.

A Station of Hope

Of course, churches that seek to be a force for healing must face the reality of the staggering number of men and women returning from incarceration and their disproportionate representation in already distressed communities. *What Shall We Then Do?* cites the U.S. Department of Justice figure that approximately 650,000 men and women were to be released from state and federal prisons in 2008—which does not include those released from city and county jails. These numbers challenge all congregations, from the Russell Streets to the Praise and Glory Tabernacles. At a recent gathering where church leaders discussed this information, emotions ranged from anger over the disproportionate numbers of African Americans incarcerated to regret that we have not stepped up our efforts to engage the returning population and their families. Virtually every church leader could share stories about how incarceration had affected families in their congregations. Yet the enormity of the problem suggests there are additional families in their congregations and communities with members in jail or prison, or in the process of reentry and reintegration.

The handbook shows how faith leaders, particularly clergy, play a critical role in helping a congregation become a Station of Hope. Clergy and other leaders provide vision for the ministry, organizational structure, and support for volunteers—but the primary persons doing the actual ministry are the laity. Becoming a Healing Community requires a change in congregational culture; therefore, leadership must provide the means of cultural change, not the primary heads, hearts, and hands of the work. Clergy can raise the issue of incarceration in a manner consistent with the ethos of the congregation—through sermons, through public prayers of intercession, and even through opportunities for testimony. The handbook notes how congregational testimonies and altar calls for those impacted by crime and the criminal justice system have "broken the silence" concerning the presence of persons affected by incarceration within many congregations. In their preaching and teaching, as well as by action, pastors set a tone of welcome and inclusion, in many cases using their own personal experiences of encountering the impact of crime and incarceration and pointing to biblical texts and examples supporting the ministry. When presenting prison ministry to congregations and church leaders, Chaplain Michael Smith often intones, "Remember, an inmate died for your sins."

Pastors and other leaders of Healing Communities seek to identify those in the congregation who are most in need of support through their experience of crime and incarceration. Within the context of a welcoming and supportive environment, others who have been burdened by shame and stigma will come forward for the support they need. The entire congregation has a roll to play in providing support networks for returning citizens and their families. As in any ministry of presence, the primary role is simply to be present and listen. Empathy and ears make for a strong universal starting point to those whose stories and pain have been hidden by shame. Church members should be prepared to welcome returning citizens without stigmatizing them, while also making space for those who return to be responsible for their actions, including some level of accountability. In creating formal and informal networks of support, church members help individuals and families to know they are heard, welcomed, and valued. Activities within these networks are often determined by the need of the moment—such as a ride to an appointment, prayers while job seeking, a meal for a family while the returning citizen is out job hunting, or financial support for bus rides and phone calls.

In learning about the realities of criminal justice and mass incarceration, congregations come to know both the structure of the system within which they must work and the challenges facing those for whom they provide assistance. Congregations should also learn about other supportive services available in their communities. Not every congregation can find or create a job for someone, but every congregation can discover what local opportunities exist for training and placement. Many locations already have existing reentry task forces, committees, and agencies operated by various government or nonprofit organizations. These should be part of the larger network into which a congregation can fit.

The families of incarcerated persons and returning citizens often require special support as well. The Amachi Mentoring Partnership is one of a number of growing agencies that provide mentoring to children of the incarcerated and training for congregations that wish to become involved in mentoring. (See chapter 5 of this book for more on this program.) Children often need assistance staying connected with incarcerated parents. In one city, African American sorority members visit the county jail and make video recordings for children of their mothers reading stories in a nursery setting. Some churches provide financial assistance to offset the expense of phone calls from a correctional facility (which can reach up to $2.50 per minute) or use church vans to shuttle family members to correctional facilities on visitation days.

One final step in the Healing Communities approach involves policy awareness and advocacy. Returning citizens often require services beyond the capacity of a local congregation. Where these structures are lacking, congregations can mobilize to advocate in both the private and public sector for their provision, energized by the knowledge that the inclusion of returning citizens and their families has brought awareness of obstacles that can only be addressed by changes in policy. Engaging in advocacy around larger systemic issues is one more way caring congregations can seek to bring healing to all who are impacted by crime and incarceration, especially those returning from prisons and jails.

▪ NOTES ▪

1. See Angelique K. Walker-Smith's excellent doctor of ministry dissertation, "Dynamics of Hospitality: The Case of Societal Reintegration of Christian Women Ex-prisoners," Princeton Theological Seminary, 1995, especially chapter one, where she makes the biblical theological case for hospitality as a framework for reentry ministry.

2. This initiative, as noted in the introduction and its footnotes, produced handbooks *Balancing Justice with Mercy* and *What Shall We Then Do?* The balance of this chapter summarizes the content of these handbooks, which are available at www.healingcommunitiesusa.org.

3. Among his many contributions to and leadership within the restorative justice movement, Howard Zehr's text *The Little Book of Restorative Justice* (Intercourse, PA: Good Books, 2002) stands out as an important precise statement on the biblical mandate for reconciliation, especially with respect to crime and criminal justice.

Chapter 16

Why Policy Matters

CHARLES E. LEWIS JR.

frican American churches can and should participate in shaping social welfare policies on the federal, state, and local levels. This is not to suggest that
our churches should establish a black version of the
Christian Coalition, which involved itself as much in
partisan politics as it did in promoting a social policy agenda.
But I am suggesting that African American churches should
participate in the process of deciding what resources are
brought to bear on some of the most troubling problems facing African Americans today. Chief among these problems is
the overrepresentation of African Americans in federal and
state criminal justice systems.

I first understood the important role churches could play
in the social policy arena in 1995 during my MSW studies
at Clark Atlanta University as I followed the various welfare
reform debates occurring in Congress and state legislatures
throughout the nation. It was apparent as these debates en-
sued that the most affected stakeholders in the process—single
mothers and their children—had very little representation at
the table. I found myself asking, "Where are the churches?"[1]

I could see then the way in which a strong collective voice from churches might influence policy-makers so that pursuit of education and more adequate childcare services would be a more significant part of the policy mix.

My intention in pursuing a degree in social work was to equip myself with the knowledge and skills that would make me an effective therapist and then return with greater capacity to my work with African American males in the church. But I quickly began to understand that while my hands-on work with the brothers was critical to their advancement, if no attention was directed at the policies impacting them—policies like mandatory sentencing and the reduction of services in prisons—we would always be fighting an uphill battle. Since I could find few people of color, I sought to acquire the skills and knowledge that would allow me to operate in the field of public policy.

The need for African American churches to involve themselves in policy advocacy was made clear to me after I returned from the Million Man March. This 1995 gathering in Washington, DC, was one of the most spectacular events in this nation's history—a massive effort that brought men, boys, and women from every corner of the country. But I found little evidence of any policy agenda emanating from this event. Eventually I found one article addressing this topic, and to my dismay it stated: "An analysis of both the official background documents and reports from the march reveals that there is no call upon national policy-makers for anything."[2] To not have a policy agenda resulting from the Million Man March was one huge missed opportunity.

Fixing Potholes on the Jericho Road

Jesus' parable of the good Samaritan is one of the great morality stories of all time is (Luke 10:30-35). In response to a lawyer's question about what is required to inherit eternal life, Jesus asks that lawyer what is written in the Scriptures. The lawyer replies, "'Love the Lord your God with all your heart and with all your soul and with all your strength and with all your mind;' and 'Love your neighbor as yourself'" (Luke 10:27, NIV). Jesus affirms the lawyer's answer then tells the parable about a man who falls into the hands of robbers and is left half dead on the road from Jerusalem to Jericho. Both a priest and a Levite walk past him, but a Samaritan stops and assists the man, tending to his wounds and paying for his stay at a nearby inn. Jesus' lesson for the lawyer is that our neighbors are often strangers in need.

Many sermons have been preached on this passage of Scripture—some pointing to the fact that the priest and Levite were traveling *down* the road toward Jericho and had probably just left worship activities in Jerusalem when they walked right passed the wounded man. Numerous ministries have been named for the good Samaritan, suggesting that it is our duty to look after those who are in distress. And well we should. But our responsibility does not end there. The church can and should continue rescuing people from the Jericho Road—helping formerly incarcerated people recover from their mistakes and trauma. But until we do something about the road and its problems, we will be continually salvaging broken people along life's Jericho Roads.

While we are tending to the needs of the suffering, we must do something to improve the conditions that cause the suffering. Perhaps policies should be put in place to ensure safer travel along the road. Perhaps we need to put lighting along the Jericho Road. Maybe we need to hire people to patrol the road. What policies are needed to provide alternatives to criminal sanctions and incarceration for nonviolent offenders? What policies can be put in place to better address the educational, psychological, and substance abuse needs of people while they are incarcerated, so they will be better suited to manage their lives once they are free to return to their communities? What policies are needed to remove barriers to successful reentry? Fixing the road will do more than trying to care for each wounded individual.

In his speech at Riverside Church shortly after returning from Israel and the Middle East, Dr. Martin Luther King Jr. stated:

> A true revolution of values will soon cause us to question the fairness and justice of many of our past and present policies. On the one hand, we are called to play the Good Samaritan on life's roadside, but that will be only an initial act. One day we must come to see that the whole Jericho Road must be transformed so that men and women will not be constantly beaten and robbed as they make their journey on life's highway. True compassion is more than flinging a coin to a beggar. It comes to see that an edifice which produces beggars needs restructuring.[3]

Advocating for policies to fix the Jericho Road does not reduce the need for ministry to incarcerated people and returning citizens. The ministries described in previous chapters that directly meet the needs of these wounded citizens are vital and should be enhanced. We need to do both. In social work this is known as addressing the needs of people *and* their environments. Attention must be given to cause as well as function. We need to assist people in functioning in the status quo but also work to ameliorate the structural and systemic challenges they face. It has been a struggle to find the right balance in our society.

The United States has long been considered the reluctant welfare state.[4] Americans take pride in being self-reliant and courageous. Our country is the land of freedom and the home of the brave. An emphasis on personal responsibility has been the order of the day, particularly during the last four decades when a strong conservative philosophy has been predominant in government. We are taught to believe individuals should rely on themselves and their families to make it in life.

The federal government's primary role is to protect us from our enemies and to limit corruption in the marketplace. The federal government does not exist to take care of us.

This translates into social welfare policies that are residual—policies that offer minimal support and only as a last resort. Social welfare policies reflect a society's philosophy about how it will provide for the welfare of its citizens. While some universal policies, such as Social Security and Medicare, are available to all citizens, most social welfare policies are means-tested and available to people with incomes below the federal poverty line. Programs such as Medicaid, food stamps, and TANF (Temporary Assistance for Needy Families) are designed to help the poor maintain a minimal subsistence.[5] We promote a society where people are expected to take advantage of the many opportunities in the United States, and it is our willingness to put in the hard work and refrain from illegal activities that ensures us a productive life. It is when we are lazy and want to depend on others and government handouts that we find ourselves at the bottom of the ladder. Hard work is rewarded; bad choices have consequences. This sounds reasonably fair until you consider that we all do not enter this world on an equal footing. Some of us were born into affluent families and healthy environments; others were not. The assumption of equal opportunity is a mostly a myth.

So what do we do with the many children born into dysfunctional households? What happens to the kid who grows up with no father or whose mother is locked behind bars? When does personal responsibility begin for a child consigned to live in a crime-ridden tenement and attend a subpar school? Do we just hope for the best—that these children will somehow escape the many pitfalls that confront them each day? Or do we create programs that will rescue those who stumble? And who pays for such programs?

That is why we have policies: to guide our thoughts and actions on how to provide for the general welfare of citizens in society, particularly those who are most vulnerable and

least able to fend for themselves. While some current policies are preventative—such as those that provide early education and support services to poor children through programs
like Head Start and WIC[6]—many policies are put into place
after problems arise. One reason we must provide support
for formerly incarcerated persons returning to communities
is because we did not quite anticipate the unintended consequences of putting so many people in prison. Put all together,
we now have a comprehensive system of social policies and
programs that qualifies us as a welfare state.

The poor in most societies—before the advent of the welfare state—were left to depend on the charity of private citizens. Traditionally, churches and other charitable organizations concerned themselves with seeing that people did not
go hungry or without clothing and shelter. It was only in the
aftermath of the Great Depression that the United States began following the lead of European nations and developed
government-run New Deal programs such as Social Security
and Aid to Dependent Children to create a safety net for the
deserving poor.[7]

While universal programs like Social Security and Medicare have become sacrosanct among American social welfare
policies, welfare or government-provided cash assistance for
the poor remains an anathema to many Americans. Public
opinion surveys bear out that Americans consistently support
efforts to help the poor yet see welfare as a program that
largely provides assistance to the "undeserving poor"—able-
bodied adults who are unwilling to fend for themselves. Research has connected these negative ideas about welfare to
the fact that many Americans have the misperception that
most poor people in the United States are black.[8]

Social welfare policies in the United States are driven in
large part by ideology. Progressives believe government has
a responsibility to provide a safety net and some minimal assistance for the poor. Conservatives believe reliance on help
from the government fosters dependency and reduces people's

motivation to do for self. They believe their mission is to protect and promote traditional American values, such as self-sufficiency and personal responsibility, and consider government welfare programs that use tax dollars to provide assistance to the poor (and "lazy) to be nothing short of highway robbery. They believe whatever help they give to the poor should be voluntary.

African American Churches and Social Welfare Policies

African American churches have always played a significant role in meeting the social welfare needs of African Americans.[9] Yet African American churches have been slow in responding to recent calls for more faith-based involvement in the social service arena.[10] Among the reasons for the slow response is the fear of having the prophetic voice of the church compromised by receiving and depending on assistance from the government. There are also concerns that many African American churches lack the organizational capacity to actively pursue and manage grants.

With that in mind, my colleague Harold Dean Trulear and I offered some ideas in an article in *Black Theology* on how churches might participate in the social service arena short of being full-fledged social service providers.[11] We encouraged churches to actively engage in policy advocacy by educating their congregations about key policy issues and helping to mobilize support for specific policy positions. African American pastors and church leaders must rely on assistance and advice from policy scholars. As a licensed minister and professional social worker, I see much opportunity for collaboration in the future.

Part of my mission since obtaining my doctorate in social policy analysis has been to promote the idea of a marriage between the religious community and the social work profession as others have done in the past.[12] In this effort, I have participated in faith-based activities and forums and worked closely with several colleagues at Howard University School of Divinity and beyond. Yet tension remains between the two camps—the religious community is concerned that spirituality will be diluted in working with the secular social work profession, while social work professionals are concerned about the lack of certification of church workers and the impact this might have on the quality of services provided. Both are valid concerns, so at this time I will forgo the idea of marriage and settle for a civil union.

In *Long March Ahead*, editor R. Drew Smith drew on the expertise of several scholars to examine the role of African American churches in the public policy arena. Because of the autonomy of many congregations and the lack of comprehensive data, it can be difficult to paint a conclusive picture on the level of involvement of African American churches in the public policy arena. Yet overall, Smith found that African American churches focus their policy advocacy on issues regarding racial justice and economic development.[13] The evidence suggested that African American pastors and churches were reluctant to weigh in on many other social issues of the day, such as welfare reform,[14] AIDS,[15] and urban education.[16]

How far churches should go in influencing policies is a matter for discussion. Someone needs to speak out for the needs of the poor. Someone must be a voice for the voiceless. There have been instances when churches speaking out have made a difference. Certainly policy gains made during the civil rights era would not have been accomplished without a major concerted effort by churches throughout the country.

What are the most critical issues of social policy confronting African Americans today? Certainly the overrepresentation in the criminal justice system deserves attention. But there are other concerns as well—health disparities, high school dropouts, HIV-AIDS. Adopting a broad policy agenda would probably be unproductive. Policy initiatives must be focused and targeted. The best approach is to develop streams of policy initiatives. Some churches will work on health-related issues, some will tackle the various aspects of disproportionate involvement in the criminal justice system, and others may focus on education. At some point, policy recommendations can be circulated via the Internet with a process for developing a consensus on policy priorities.

Reforming Criminal Justice

There are many valuable policy ideas and proposals seeking to reduce the involvement of adults and youth in the criminal justice system that deserve consideration. Churches can decide which of these initiatives deserve their support:

The Second Chance Act of 2007: Community Safety through Recidivism Prevention, sponsored by Rep. Danny K. Davis of Illinois, was passed by the House in November 2007 and signed into law by President George W. Bush on April 9, 2008, becoming Public Law 110-199. The law was enacted to provide support to formerly incarcerated people returning to their communities. Although the bill passed the House by a wide margin and was approved by unanimous consent in the Senate, several key provisions in the original legislation were omitted from the final law, such as exoneration of prison records for nonviolent offenders after an extended period with no criminal activities. While the law received bipartisan support, appropriations for the law ($25 million for fiscal year 2009) fell far short of the $165 million authorized in the original legislation. The Obama Administration sought $100 million for Second Chance Act programs for fiscal year 2011. Churches could push for more funding for the legislation.

At the time of this writing, the Youth PROMISE Act (Prison Reduction through Opportunities, Mentoring, Intervention, Support and Education) sponsored by Rep. Bobby

Scott of Virginia, was on a slow track making its way through Congress. The Youth PROMISE Act would provide funding and resources to communities with severe gang problems that would enable them to create neighborhood youth coordinating councils that would bring together key stakeholders to assess and intervene with evidence-based programs. The bill supports programs designed to reduce gang-related activities, promote positive youth development, and help strengthen families and communities. Should the bill become law, the Congressional Budget Office (CBO) estimates its cost at $1.9 billion over five years.

Michael Jacobson, executive director of the Vera Institute and former commissioner of the New York City Departments of Correction and Probation and a deputy budget director for the City of New York in the Koch, Dinkins, and Giuliani administrations, offers some interesting policy ideas for restructuring parole systems in his book *Downsizing Prisons*. He proposes moving parole resources up front, spending a large amount on a parolee in the first year following his or her release to provide services to help the formerly incarcerated person successfully transition back into the community. He also suggests using risk level instruments to determine the level of supervision for each parolee and decreasing resources after the initial investment.[17]

While supporting specific legislation is certainly worthwhile, policy positions are equally important, and the wellspring from which specific policies and legislation will flow. For example, we might contend that all children and youth are entitled to engage in athletics and the arts regardless of the abilities of their families and communities to fund and provide access to these activities. Such policy is rooted in the belief that exposing children and adolescents to music and art and providing safe places for them to exercise and participate in team sports is a social good that produces well-rounded youth and enhances their chances of escaping crime and making contributions to society. Ensuring that poor children have access to comparable opportunities offered affluent children is what it means to level the playing field.

Finally, churches can play a role in how necessary programs are funded. With the Reagan and Bush tax cuts, more money has moved into the hands of private citizens; this means private investments may be required to sustain valuable programs that were started with public dollars. With rigorously evaluated programs and interventions, churches and nonprofit organizations can provide vehicles for the successful—particularly those who "escaped" disadvantaged neighborhoods—to give back. Let's start the conversation and see where it leads.

■ NOTES ■

1. Megan E. McLaughlin, "The Role of African American Churches in Crafting the 1996 Welfare Reform Policy," in *Long March Ahead: African Americans and Public Policy in Post-Civil Rights America*, ed. R. Drew Smith, 58–59 (Durham, NC: Duke University Press, 2004).

2. Hanes Walton Jr., "Public Policy Responses to the Million Man March," *The Black Scholar* 25, no. 4 (2001): 19.

3. Martin Luther King Jr., "Beyond Vietnam—A Time to Break Silence," speech delivered April 4, 1967, at Riverside Church (New York), American Rhetoric Online Speech Bank, http://www.american rhetoric.com/speeches/mlkatimetobreaksilence.htm (accessed April 9, 2010).

4. Bruce S. Jansson, *The Reluctant Welfare State: Engaging History to Advance Social Work Practice in Contemporary Society* (Pacific Grove, CA: Brooks Cole, 2008), 525.

5. The work-based program Temporary Assistance for Needy Families (TANF) replaced the entitlement program Aid to Families with Dependent Children (AFDC) in 1996 with the passage of PUB. L. 104-193, the Personal Responsibility and Work Reconciliation Act (PRWORA). The new TANF program instituted a work requirement and time limits for assistance that were determined by states; however, participants were limited to no more than five years of federal assistance.

6. WIC was established in 1972 as a pilot program to provide food, nutrition counseling, and access to health services to low-income women, infants, and children under the Special Supplemental Nutrition Program for Women, Infants, and Children. WIC was made permanent in 1974 and is administered by the Food and Nutrition Service of the U.S. Department of Agriculture. Formerly known as the Special Supplemental Food Program

for Women, Infants, and Children, WIC's name was changed under the Healthy Meals for Healthy Americans Act of 1994 in order to emphasize its role as a nutrition program. Most state WIC programs provide vouchers that participants use at authorized food stores. A wide variety of state and local organizations cooperate in providing the food and health care benefits, and 46,000 merchants nationwide accept WIC vouchers.

7. The deserving poor were considered to be the blind, the disabled, widows, the elderly, children, and people who fell on tough economic times through no fault of their own (i.e., death of a spouse, layoffs, etc.).

8. Martin Gilens, *Why Americans Hate Welfare: Race, Media, and the Policy of Antipoverty Policies* (Chicago: University of Chicago Press, 1999), 2–4.

9. See the following for a historical perspective on African American churches and social welfare services: E. Franklin Frazier, *The Negro Church in America* (New York: Schocken, 1969); C. Eric Lincoln and Lawrence H. Mamiya, *The Black Church in the African American Experience* (Durham, NC: Duke University Press, 1990); and Andrew Billingsley, *Mighty Like a River: The Black Church and Social Reform* (Oxford: Oxford University Press, 1990).

10. David A. Bositis, *Black Churches and the Faith-Based Initiative: Findings from a National Survey* (Washington, DC: Joint Center for Political and Economic Studies, 2006), 7–8.

11. Charles E. Lewis Jr., and Harold Dean Trulear, "Rethinking the Role of African American Churches as Social Service Providers," *Black Theology* 6, no. 3 (2008).

12. Robert Wineberg, "Relationships between Religions and Social Services: An Arranged Marriage or A Renewal of Vows," *Social Work and Christianity* 23, no. 1 (1996): 24–25.

13. R. Drew Smith, *Long March Ahead: African American Churches and Public Policy in the Post-Civil Rights America* (Durham, NC: Duke University Press, 2004).

14. McLaughlin, "Role of African American Churches," 59.

15. Cathy J. Cohen, "Service Provider or Policymaker? Black Churches and the Health of African Americans," in *Long March Ahead: African Americans and Public Policy in Post-Civil Rights America*, ed. R. Drew Smith, 118–19 (Durham, NC: Duke University Press, 2004).

16. Desiree Pedescleaux, "African American Clergy and Urban School Reform," in *Long March Ahead: African Americans and Public Policy in Post-Civil Rights America*, ed. R. Drew Smith, 162–64 (Durham, NC: Duke University Press, 2004).

17. Michael Jacobson, *Downsizing Prisons: How to Reduce Crime and End Mass Incarceration* (New York: New York University Press, 2005), 166–69.

The Way Forward

W. WILSON GOODE SR., CHARLES E. LEWIS JR., AND HAROLD DEAN TRULEAR

Ours is an imperfect society in an imperfect world. Many problems need to be addressed in our nation and our communities. But none is more threatening to the health and well-being of African Americans than our disproportionate involvement in the criminal justice system. Involvement in the criminal justice system scars and disrupts the lives of millions of children, adults, and families. What can African American churches do to help reduce the rate of incarceration of African Americans? Why should they act?

Churches were established to bring people to God and some order to the world. In bringing people to God, our hope is to help people live abundantly in the midst of chaos. And in the process of bringing people to salvation, the Christian church is charged with alleviating suffering—preaching good news to the impoverished, healing the brokenhearted, liberating those in captivity, and providing sight where there is none (Luke 4:18). Throughout this book, the authors have painstakingly detailed the impact of incarceration on the lives and communities of African Americans and highlighted some of the responses churches have made to address this menace. Although the pace of annual increase in the incarceration rate has slowed, the problem remains.

Two decades ago the black community was up in arms over the fact that one of every four African American men between the ages of twenty and twenty-nine was involved in the criminal justice system. Articles were being written about the plight of young black males and the notion they were an "endangered species." Today one in three young African American males is under supervision of the criminal justice system, despite millions of dollars spent on research and programs addressing the problem.

We know a great deal about the people who get caught up in the criminal justice system. They are more likely to be substance abusers. They are more likely to struggle with mental illnesses, both diagnosed and undiagnosed. They are more likely to be high school dropouts with poor labor market skills. They are more likely to grow up in poor neighborhoods rife with crime and drugs and patrolled by an overaggressive police force. Hundreds, if not thousands, of studies have been done on the prison population and their families and communities.

We have learned much about children who are most at risk of getting involved in the criminal justice system: they are black and poor; they are children of the incarcerated; they are academically deficient; they are in foster care; they are socially isolated; and they have psychological, emotional, and behavioral problems. Many are growing up in households without a father or with a mother overwhelmed by any number of social and economic challenges.

Having overcome slavery and state-sponsored discrimination, the African American community must devote itself to undoing the overrepresentation of its people in the criminal justice system. This is the civil rights struggle for the twenty-first century. The goal of dramatically reducing the numbers of African Americans engaged on all levels of the criminal justice system will not be easily accomplished. Just like the civil rights struggles of years past, reducing our involvement in the criminal justice system will take a movement. Churches must decide what their role will be in this new crusade.

Uniting Faith and Action

So what makes us believe churches can make a difference? We believe churches are critical because there is a spiritual dimension to the disproportionate involvement of African Americans in the criminal justice system, and it is a dimension that remains unaddressed by government officials and policy-makers. Jesus spoke of demons that could be overcome only by prayer and fasting (Mark 9:29), and this is exactly that type of problem. Prayer and fasting alone will not reduce the inexorable march of young African American boys and girls into a system designed to devour the spirit and the body. But prayer and fasting will empower us to find solutions to this vexing problem.

Churches are our best and maybe our only hope of reducing the numbers of African Americans involved in the criminal justice system. No amount of social programs or interventions will turn things around. It will take faith and action. But before we can get to faith, there must be a will on the part of young people to want to stay out of the criminal justice system. There must be a desire on their part to excel in school and pursue lifestyles that respect social norms and reject the temptations of drugs and crime.

Our children must repent. It is the prerequisite for healing. When Jesus encountered the afflicted, his first question was not, "Do you have faith?" His first question was, "Do you want to be healed? Faith can be applied only when there is a desire for healing." Without that desire and commitment for a new reality, change will not happen. Churches must help our children see there is another way. Then we must use our collective voices and political strength to demand that adequate resources are available to provide for the needs of children.

Children and youth must have access to productive activities that enhance their growth and human capital development. More often than not, poor children in both rural and urban areas are not offered the opportunities their more affluent peers have to experience arts and culture. They are left to television, movies, and video games, while other kids have additional opportunities to attend the theater, participate in music and dance, practice musical instruments, learn chess, and play on neighborhood soccer and baseball teams. The more positive social activities young people can participate in the less time they will have for risky and delinquent behaviors.

Providing programs and activities for young people is expensive. As state and federal budgets for defense, older Americans (Social Security, Medicare), crime control, and prisons continue to rise unabated, fewer resources are being devoted to providing these kinds of activities for young people. Congress passed the Juvenile Justice and Delinquency Prevention Act (JJDPA) in 1974 to assist states in generating the resources needed to create activities that would reduce the chances of underprivileged youth getting caught up in the juvenile justice system.[1] However, these programs took a severe hit with the 2002 reauthorization of the act by a Republican-led Congress and during the Bush administration—both operating on the conservative philosophy that raising children is not the job of government and is best left in the hands of parents. This reauthorization bundled a number of programs into a Juvenile Delinquency Prevention Block Grant for which funding was never appropriated. The budget for the Office of Juvenile Justice and Delinquency Prevention (OJJDP), which had remained stable at about $550 million from 1999 to 2002, was cut to $348 million by 2007, a reduction of 38 percent.[2] While the cost of preventing young people from going into the criminal justice system may seem exorbitant, the monetary value of keeping even one high-risk youth out of the system is in the range of $2.6 to $4.4 million, when the costs of criminal justice and loss of productivity are included.[3]

Churches must open their arms and their doors to those who are already caught in the system yet wanting to pursue other paths in life. We must not only minister to those who are currently incarcerated and welcome returning citizens into the fellowship, but also advocate to ensure that adequate housing, employment, and social services are in place to meet the needs of these individuals who must endure the stigma and impediments for the rest of their lives. This means paying attention to policy as much as programs. This means aligning forces with people of goodwill in various sectors of public and private society.

There are, of course, downsides for churches in "partnering with Caesar."[4] The greatest fear is the loss of our prophetic voice. It is difficult, if not impossible, to speak truth to power when the funding you need to continue providing social services comes from those you need to hold accountable. This is especially true when you are dependent upon Caesar for resources to provide critical services to people who desperately need those services. Do you risk eliminating those services in order to hold a key politician or administrator's feet to the fire?

Social justice and social ministry must be the order of the day. Most churches and pastors are not of the mind-set to engage the political and policy-making systems on behalf of people in the crosshairs of the criminal justice system. Many church leaders lack the means to successfully engage secular institutions to make change. There are few mechanisms to galvanize their collective voices. However, clear vision and faithful activism of churches is exactly what is needed to engage a criminal justice system that seems bereft of compassion for those who have fallen or are getting left behind. The ideas for change will come from churches. We must think our way out of this mess.

When Jesus said future generations would do even greater things than he had done (John 14:12)—his prognostication was not restricted to the laying on of hands and healing of the sick and troubled. It means we have much more at our disposal to do the work of the Lord. The use of current technologies must not be limited to war, entertainment, and other secular activities. It is incumbent on church people to use technology to fulfill our biblical mandates. Websites are ubiquitous within the church community. But are we using this technology to connect children and families to the help they need to keep our kids out of the juvenile justice system? Can the formerly incarcerated find the vital information they need that could keep them afloat?

Some will argue that this is not a job for churches—that child welfare, juvenile justice, and reentry programs are better left to the government. They may see the church's job as bringing souls to God, giving alms to the needy, and praying for redemption. Yet Dr. King warned about such complacency in his book *Strength to Love*:

> We preachers have also been tempted by the enticing cult of conformity. Seduced by the success symbols of the world, we have measured our achievements by the size of our parsonage. We have become showmen to please the whims and caprices of the people. We preach comforting sermons and avoid saying anything from our pulpit which might disturb the respectable views of the comfortable members of our congregations. Have we ministers of Jesus Christ sacrificed truth on the altar of self-interest and, like Pilate, yielded our convictions to the demands of the crowd?[5]

Morehouse College president Robert M. Franklin has written about his participation in a campaign to address disproportionate African American involvement in the criminal justice system that began with great fanfare and great promise yet soon "expended its energy, never to be heard from again."[6] He says many such efforts lack a multidisciplinary approach—that "village leaders" feel they can accomplish more by focusing their efforts within the arena where they are most knowledgeable. In *Crisis in the Village*, Franklin lays out a six-step plan that begins with focused conversation, requires collaborative leadership, develops a vision and plan, demands accountability and action, calls for developing resources, and leads to documenting and celebrating progress.[7]

Ultimately, if churches want to find solutions to prevent young people from going astray, they must find the wherewithal to engage young people and provide structures that allow them to participate in a meaningful way. A recent Pew Center poll of millennials (young Americans between the ages of eighteen and twenty-nine) found that 68 percent self-identified as Christian—10 percent less than the overall population.[8] However, those who are people of faith are as fervent about their faith as previous generations.[9] In fact, compared to previous generations when they were the same age, a greater percentage of millennials believe houses of worship should speak out on social issues.[10] Almost six in ten (57 percent) reported volunteering in their communities, about the same as previous generations.[11]

To attract and keep young people, churches must provide programming that will be relevant to their needs. Traditionally, African American churches have sought to attract young people with religiously focused activities (youth choir, youth services, Bible studies, lectures, and films). A survey of 635 northern African American churches by sociologist Andrew Billingsley found that 176 of these churches provided nontraditional youth-related activities—primarily teen support, sports activities, financial aid for students, parenting and sexuality programs, and youth substance abuse programs.[12]

It will not be easy to effect change in a prison-industrial complex that is deeply entrenched in our society. In the end, it will take a movement of African Americans across all generations to get the job done. While this problem is not of our making, we must own it. If we cannot stop the flow of children going into the criminal justice abyss, we will be doing reentry programs in perpetuity. Our churches have the moral imperative to lead the fight against mass incarceration, seeking allies in various sectors of society, with the understanding that the present system destroys the body and the soul. If Jesus came that all of God's children might have a path to an abundant life and salvation from eternal death, then neither the prison gates nor the gates of hell can prevail.

▪ NOTES ▪

1. The federal government often raises funds for education and needed social programs that are traditionally left to the jurisdiction of states, because states struggle to raise these funds while competing with each other to keep taxes low in order to attract business and a viable workforce.

2. Blas Nunez-Neto, "Juvenile Justice Funding Trends" (Washington, DC: Congressional Research Service, Order Code RS22655, 2007) http://assets.opencrs.com/rpts/RS22655_20070427.pdf (accessed March 18, 2010).

3. Mark A. Cohen and Alex R. Piquero, "New Evidence on the Value of Saving a High Risk Youth," *Journal of Quantitative Criminology* 25 (2009): 46.

4. See Michael Leo Owens, *God and Government in the Ghetto: The Politics of Church-State Collaboration in Black America* (Chicago: University of Chicago Press, 2007), 118–20.

5. Martin Luther King, Jr., *Strength to Love* (Cleveland, OH: Collins + World, 1997), 25.

6. Robert M. Franklin, *Crisis in the Village: Restoring Hope in African American Communities* (Minneapolis: Augsburg Fortress, 2007), 23.

7. Ibid., 229–38.

8. Pew Research Center, "The Millennials: A Portrait of Generation Next" (Washington, DC: Author), 87, http://pewresearch.org/millennials/ (accessed March 18, 2010).

9. Ibid., 89.

10. Ibid., 106.

11. Ibid., 83.

12. Andrew Billingsley, Ph.D., *Mighty Like a River* (New York: Oxford University Press), 91, 217.

Afterword

DEEDEE M. COLEMAN

Once again African American churches are confronted with a societal challenge that seems insurmountable. Born in the fields of slave hands, our churches led the way to emancipation from slavery, fought back Jim Crow laws, provided leadership in the halls of Congress, and helped to elect an African American—President Barack Obama—to the White House. At some point in time, each of these challenges seemed improbable, if not impossible. But through the grace of God and the faith of mothers and fathers praying, marching, and taking bold actions, we have made significant progress in these United States.

Yet much of what we have accomplished with our ancestors' blood, sweat, and tears is threatened today by the tsunami of a criminal justice system that threatens to swallow up more and more African Americans—particularly our men and our young. After decades of countless plans and programs, we again must look to the church for our salvation. For if history has taught us anything, it is that Jesus never fails! When we decide that we *want* to be healed and we believe that we *can* be healed, Jesus will provide everything we need.

The book you are now holding, *Ministry with Prisoners & Families: The Way Forward*, embraces a wealth of information that revolves around restoration and forgiveness. These resources of hope have the potential to transform the lives of returning citizens who are burdened with stigma upon coming back to their communities after incarceration, even as they seek opportunities for change. In working with the offender population for the last thirty-two years, I have found that the words on these pages challenge us—with no middle ground. Either we put the stigma aside and follow the mandate of God with courage, accepting our role in pursuing forgiveness for those who desire to provide restitution to God and society for their past history, or we dare not venture into the lives of those who cannot afford another setback. This book encourages us to take a look at the approaches of those who are doing the work of reentry.

As chair of the Progressive National Baptist Convention's Commission on Social Justice and Prison Ministry, I often ask the question, "What more can I do?" As I journeyed through these writings, I realize the question is not what more can I do, but what am I doing *right now* to make humanity better? The authors and scholars of this book draw you into accountability for the work of restoration with those who have had soul-searching changes that affect their lives in a transforming way. This book is unique, not because of its diverse subject matter in dealing with stigma and change of the returning citizen, but because it testifies to the powerful results of real reentry ministries. It reveals also the heart and work of individuals who dare to make a difference in the way people should be treated.

This book will serve as a reference for every person who desires not only to do the work of healing, but to be a carrier of the Word of God and to cherish every man and woman afflicted with the stain of incarceration. Well done!

DeeDee M. Coleman, BA, MA, DD
Chair, Progressive National Baptist Convention
Commission on Social Justice and Prison Ministry

Name and Subject Index

advocacy ministry, 11
African Americans in criminal justice system
    disproportionate numbers of, 19, 20, 48, 58
    implications for the African American church, 46–47, 53–55
    reasons for, 46, 47–53
Amachi mentoring, 68–73, 177
Annie E. Casey Foundation, 2, 63
Anti–Drug Abuse Act of 1988, 111

Big Brothers Big Sisters of America, 69, 70. *See also* Amachi; Mentoring of
        children of incarcerated parents
Breaking the Chain model, 75–81
Brown, Rhozier "Roach" Brown, 133
Burglass, Milton "Mickey," 51
Bush, George W., 27, 71, 99, 187, 194

California Correctional Peace Officers Association, 26–27
chaplain
    as church trainer, 160–62, 166–68
    as liaison between inmates and churches, 165–66
    as minister to families, 163–65
    as pastor to prisoner, 159–60
    responsibilities of, 158–59
    role of, 6–7, 34, 156–57
Chester, Pennsylvania, 44, 45, 52, 54
children
    connections with parent during parental incarceration, 125–27
    effects of parental incarceration on, 9, 22, 58, 64, 66–73, 74–75,
        120–27
    preventative measures with, 93–94
    See also Amachi; Families, effects of incarceration of family members
        on; Juvenile justice system; Mentoring of children of incarcerated
        parents
Christian Association for Prisoner Aftercare, 91
Christian correctional ministry
    equipping of professionals and volunteers for, 34–43
    scriptural basis for, 32–33
church's attitude toward returning citizens, 142–51

About the Contributors

Owen C. Cardwell Jr., MDiv, is a PhD student in the MLK Inter-disciplinary Studies program at Union Institute and University in Cincinnati, Ohio. He also is pastor and founder of New Canaan International Church in Richmond, Virginia, and executive director of New Jubilee Educational and Family Life Center, Inc.

Elwood Gray Jr., MDiv, DMin (earned), was ordained by the First Baptist Church of Raleigh, North Carolina. Dr. Gray is presently Pastor of Peace in the Valley Baptist Church in Silver Spring, Maryland, and founder and president of the National Coalition of Prison Ministries. He holds membership with the American Correctional Association, Howard University School of Divinity Alumni Association, the National Association for the Advancement of Colored People, and the Black Ministers Conference of Montgomery County, Maryland.

Deborah Jackson-Meyers, DMin, was ordained by the Sabbath Day Adventist Agape SDA Church of Brooklyn, New York. Elder Dr. Jackson-Meyers serves on the pastoral staff of the Upperroom Fellowship Center of Columbia, Maryland, and is founder and executive director of Breaking the Chain Foundation.

Veronica Crawford Lynch, MSW, PhD, received her graduate and postgraduate degrees from Howard University School of Social Work. She is a member of Metropolitan Baptist Church in Washington, DC, and is currently working as a program evaluation research consultant for a child welfare agency in Baltimore, Maryland.

Madeline McClenney-Sadler, MDiv, PhD, holds her doctorate in religion (Hebrew Bible) from Duke University and a master's from Howard University. Dr. McClenney-Sadler is president and founder of Exodus Foundation.org, a reentry ministry with a national and global vision. She was ordained in the Baptist tradition and is currently a member of Mt. Carmel Baptist Church in Charlotte, North Carolina.

The late Lonnie McLeod Jr., MDiv, DMin, was ordained in the United Church of Christ and served as senior pastor of the Church of the Living Hope in East Harlem, New York. Dr. McLeod also served as president of the Exodus Transitional Community, Inc. He was an accomplished public speaker, a counselor to emotionally challenged youth, and a social and criminal justice activist.

Sylvia Moseley-Robinson, MDiv, was ordained at Omega Baptist Church where she serves as associate minister and leader of the social justice ministry. Currently enrolled in the Payne Bakke Doctor of Ministry Transformational Leadership program, Rev. Moseley-Robinson is also director of the Montgomery County Volunteer Jail Chaplaincy Ministry, board member of Oasis House Ministry (which assists women trapped in the sex industry), and employee of Goodwill Easter Seals Miami Valley Ex-Offender Reentry Program.

Keith Reeves, PhD, is associate professor of political science and public policy and faculty director of the Center for Social and Policy Studies at Swarthmore College. He teaches decision-making skills to incarcerated black males in several Pennsylvania correctional institutions and is author of *Voting Hopes or Fears?* and the forthcoming *The Declining Significance of Black Males*.

Alfreda "Frieda" Robinson-Dawkins is a tireless advocate for women in the criminal justice system, after enduring the same system for ten years. She holds master's degrees in special education and counseling and currently directs the National Women's Prison Project in Baltimore, Maryland. A member of the Calvary Baptist Church and a Weinberg Fellow, she is a global trainer and Offender Workforce Development Specialist (OWDS).

Michael R. Smith Sr., MDiv, D.Min., was ordained in the American Baptist Churches USA. He has served as prison chaplain in state and federal prisons for more than twenty years. Dr. Smith is founder of Cross of Christ Ministries, which trains and educates churches in responding to crime and incarceration and promotes biblical discipleship.

Karen K. Swanson, EdD, is director of the Institute for Prison Ministries at the Billy Graham Center, Wheaton College, and assistant professor in the Christian formation and ministries department. Dr. Swanson serves at Blanchard Alliance Church, Warrenville, Illinois, and is coauthor of *Coming Home! A Guide for Those Receiving a Loved One Back from Prison or Jail*.

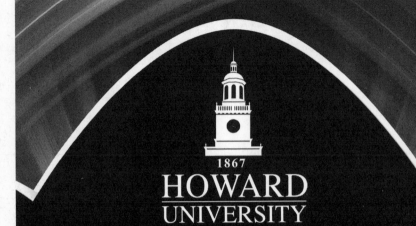

HOWARD
UNIVERSITY
School of Divinity

Pursuing Excellence in Scholarship and Ministry

1400 Shepherd St. NE
Washington DC 20017
www.divinity.howard.edu

Recognizing that the biggest impediment to effective work is a cramped vision, Christian leaders in Philadelphia chose to commit themselves to invest in the leaders who are engaged in effective, Christ-centered solutions and to initiate change in under-served areas such as church division, neighborhood blight and educational short-comings. Therefore, in 1983 the Philadelphia Leadership Foundation (PLF) was born to serve as a vehicle through which the answers to these issues could be addressed. PLF's mission is to serve as a catalyst to bring people, government, businesses and others together in the interest of enhancing the quality of life of individuals and families in the Philadelphia region. To learn more, visit: www.philadelphialeadershipfoundation.org.

PLF PROGRAMS

PLF offers programs that have both local and national significance in areas of mentoring, prisoner reintegration, nonprofit capacity building and local partnership. These include:

- ◊ AMACHI Mentoring Coalition Project
- ◊ Community Impact Institute
- ◊ Healing Communities
- ◊ Urban Coalition
- ◊ Religious Leaders Council